GOURMET INSPIRATIONS

"The Art of Healthy Cooking"

by

Patti Lynch

Published by
Sweet Inspirations Publishing

Boehringer Mannheim Corporation, the maker of Accu-Chek® Blood Glucose Monitors, wants to thank you for your purchase. Please enjoy your new *Gourmet Inspirations* cookbook with our thanks and wishes for many healthy, tasty meals.

 *Diagnostics*

Accu-Chek®
BLOOD GLUCOSE MONITORING SYSTEMS
What it takes to take control

To Mom and Dad,
who taught me that all
of my failures were only
stepping stones to success.

Thank You with Love

SWEET INSPIRATIONS PUBLISHING
1420 NW GILMAN BLVD #2258
ISSAQUAH, WASHINGTON 98027

Printed in Hong Kong

Second Printing: 1995

ISBN 0-9620469-1-4

TABLE OF CONTENTS

REVIEWS

Love your new book!

The chatty descriptions, hints, and suggestions
make it so warm and homey.

The recipes are so bright, flavorful, and new!!
Another winner!

Thanks so much!

Nancy J.V. Bohannon, M.D.
Endocrinology, Diabetes, Internal Medicine
San Francisco, California

REVIEWS

As a practicing registered dietitian, I have often wished for one cookbook that I could recommend to all my clients. I think Patti Lynch has, in this cookbook, granted my wish!

As I worked to provide the nutritional information that accompanies these recipes, it became apparent that Patti's creativity and concern for good health have worked together to provide a unique collection of recipes. This one cookbook manages to:

- include a good balance of old fashioned comfort foods, updated to the nutrition of the 90's, along with many favorites of today's generation.

- use ingenious ways to reduce fat.

- focus on a wide variety of fresh vegetables, grains, and beans to encourage more fiber.

- reduce sodium content of recipes to fit into most sodium restricted diets.

- de-emphasize desserts while providing a variety of fruit sweetened favorites to round out any meal.

I look forward to providing this cookbook as a practical tool for my clients as well as using it as a source of new, good tasting, healthy recipes for my family. Thanks, Patti.

Margaret O'Leary, RD CDE
Buse Diabetes Center
Virginia Mason Medical Center
Seattle, Washington

ACKNOWLEDGMENTS

I wish to thank my dear friend, Chris Collins, for the beautiful cover and dividers she created for GOURMET INSPIRATIONS. As an art broker, I have worked with Chris for over 10 great years. Her paintings are found in collections all over the world. Many of her large English Garden paintings can be seen in the Nordstrom Store collections across the country from Washington D.C. to Chicago to Los Angeles. Her work is truly exquisite and a treat for the eyes. Chris is a world class artist and a wonderful person, always balancing her careers as wife, mother, and artist to perfection.

I wish to thank Margaret O'Leary RD, CDE, for her advice, guidance, and direction, in my latest project: GOURMET INSPIRATIONS. In addition to analyzing the recipes, Margaret recommended ways to clarify ingredients and directions to make the book flow smoothly. Thank you, Margaret, for your interest and your many hours.

I certainly do thank my husband, Ron, for the hours he spent in proof-reading, and providing moral support and encouragement.

Thanks also to Joe Lowder of Communication Architects for editing, layout, and typesetting services.

RECIPE ANALYSIS

The software program used to analyze the recipes in GOURMET INSPIRATIONS was "Nutritionist III, version 7.0" from N2 Computing, Salem, Oregon. Data not included in that data base was obtained primarily from manufacturers.

The following assumptions are made in the nutrition information provided with each recipe:

1. "Optional" ingredients are not included in the nutrition information unless stated in the recipe.

2. All broth or stock is assumed to be salt free.

3. "Tr" means "trace" and indicates less than .6 grams or less than 5 milligrams of the stated nutrient.

4. When turkey or chicken is called for, the cooked or raw weight given with the recipe is used to determine nutrition information.

CREATING RECIPES
WITH FRUIT SWEETENERS

Converting a recipe which requires sugar to a fruit sweet-ened recipe is not always simple. Fruit sweetener is twice as sweet tasting as sugar, so only half as much is required. For example, if a recipe calls for 1 cup of sugar, replace it with 1/2 cup of fruit sweetener. This may need to be adjusted slightly, but it is difficult to say until the recipe has been made.

Keep in mind that sugar melts then hardens as it cooks. Fruit sweetener in the liquid form remains a liquid. For this reason you will probably need to leave out some of the liquid called for in a recipe. With cakes, you could cut back on some of the milk or liquid normally required. You may leave out an egg yolk, which will also cut down on the fat and cholesterol.

BAKING TIME

Reduce the baking time on your dessert or bread. This is also experimental, as all ovens are different. For cookies and bars, I usually reduce the time 10-15 minutes. Cookies should be just set; sometimes they take as little as five minutes to bake. Muffins also take much less time. I usually bake muffins in my oven for 10 minutes. Breads, bar cookies, cakes, and bundt cakes are a little tricky. I have tested all of the recipes in my oven; however, depending on the type of pan used, I may alter the time or temperature. If I bake a cake in a bundt pan that I normally bake in a 9" x 13" pan, I may want to reduce the heat slightly and bake the cake a bit longer to insure the center of the cake getting done. Like all cakes, the center is a bit more moist than the edges.

One of the best things about using fruit sweeteners rather than sugar is that the end products are very moist (unless over-baked ... and then they are VERY dry!) and they keep in Tupperware type containers in the refrigerator for a long time. Also, they stay moist. A sugar product will dry out quickly in the refrigerator.

FRUIT SWEETENERS vs HONEY, RICE SYRUP

Honey and fruit sweeteners look similar, but honey contains glucose that normally causes a fast and high rise in the blood sugar. Honey is 75% as sweet tasting as table sugar. To get the sweetening power of sugar, you would have to add 1 1/4 times as much honey as sugar. Rice syrup based sweeteners also cause a fast rise in the blood sugar. It also is less sweet tasting than sugar. It reacts in the body much like corn syrup. If you have a condition such as diabetes, honey and rice syrup may not be appropriate to use. Fructose is a naturally occurring sugar found in fruit (there is also some fructose in honey) that is not associated with a rapid rise in blood sugar. Because fructose is twice as sweet tasting as table sugar, less is used in a recipe. This provides a double benefit ... fewer calories, more sweetness.

The most important thing to remember is that you must be responsible when you include any desserts, sugars, or fats in your meal plan, especially if you have a condition such as high cholesterol or diabetes.

My recipes are designed to help people who desire no refined sugar in their diets to be able to enjoy a more normal life-style with treats that are easy and delicious.

OIL, EGGS, and HYDROGENATED FAT

In recipes, such as breads and muffins, I usually use oil. When I bake for my family, I often replace half of the oil or margarine in bar cookies, muffins, and breads with non-fat yogurt. (This is assuming a recipe calls for approximately 1/2 cup margarine.) If a recipe calls for as little as 2 Tablespoons margarine or oil, I use precisely that amount. If you cut the fat down too much, your end product may be dry and tasteless.

I also eliminate egg yolks and, when I think it necessary, I may add an extra egg white or a bit of non-fat yogurt. This will cut down on the fat calories. It, obviously, is not the kind of thing that works well in a pastry recipe. It is very difficult to lower the oil or margarine in a pastry recipe without making the pastry tough. I do, however, roll the pastry dough as thin as I possibly can so each serving has a thin flaky crust with as little fat as possible.

Be cautious about using products containing hydrogenated fats. Hydrogenation is a process which causes a fat to become saturated. One example may be a product that claims to have no tropical oils or cholesterol, yet the fat used in it is hydrogenated. When selecting a margarine, be sure that the first ingredient is an oil and not a hydrogenated oil.

FAT FREE PRODUCTS

Be careful when using fat free cream cheese, fat free ricotta, or tub margarines in baking. Some of these products may work in some recipes, but usually not. The cream cheese and ricotta have fillers so they do not hold up under heat and your cheesecake may be flat. The tub margarines usually have water as their first ingredient, which is why they have less calories per tsp. It is better to replace part of the fat with non fat yogurt (which does work), apple sauce, or pureed prunes. Just remember, you are adding more simple carbohydrates with the fruits. The fat free products are fine to use in snacks or as spreads!

FUDGE TOPPINGS

My favorite fudge toppings are the Wax Orchards products. They are extremely low in fat. They are very thick and can be thinned slightly with a small amount of low-fat evaporated milk. This is helpful when using the fudge as a frosting or a drizzle.

HELPFUL HINTS

I always combine the margarine and fruit sweetener together in a small plastic bowl and place it in the microwave for about 25 seconds on medium high. This way the ingredients are well blended with no lumps of margarine. It is, actually, much faster to use fruit sweeteners in baking because you do not have to spend a lot of time creaming the margarine and sugar.

I, also, sometimes use 1 tsp. butter in place of 1 tsp. margarine in a recipe. Just a tiny bit of butter does add lots of flavor. Remember, however, you know your own needs. If your cholesterol is out of check, do not do this.

HINTS ABOUT INGREDIENTS

One of the best investments I have made is the book: THE COMPLETE BOOK OF FOOD COUNTS by Corinne Netzer. It is a great reference book listing fat, sodium, protein, fiber, carbohydrate, cholesterol, and calorie count on many foods. Many items are listed by brand names to help the average consumer select the healthiest foods for general and specific needs. There are a number of books on this subject. With the many new products entering the marketplace, it is helpful to have a current copy.

MEAT

I would encourage each of you to become educated about which meats are lowest in fat. Here are a few figures which may be helpful:

Turkey; dark meat, no skin	3 oz.	159 calories	6.13 grams fat
Turkey; breast, no skin	3 oz.	114 calories	.62 grams fat
Turkey; skin only	1 oz.	125 calories	11.26 grams fat
Beef; ground, lean	3 oz.	227 calories	15.60 grams fat

This is one of the reasons I mix ground turkey breast and beef in my meat loaf.

SODIUM

Sodium is in nearly every packaged product in our super-markets. Many companies are responding to our dietary desires by bringing out low salt versions of soups and sauces. I use bread crumbs in a number of my recipes. Unfortunately, many of the grocery store brands are high in sodium. If this is a problem in your diet, you may choose to make your own. (I know... when do I have time to make bread crumbs? I don't have time to make toast!)

RICE AND GRAINS

Some of the tastiest and most nutritious combinations are mixed grains, pastas, and beans.

Wheat Berry

I have used wheat berry in place of beans in one of my chili recipes. If you cannot find wheat berry, you may substitute barley. Wheat berry is also great in bread, soups, or combined with rice, pasta, or beans. Wheat berries must be soaked 8 hours or overnight. After soaking, rinse well and cook in a large saucepan in 1 1/2 quarts water. Bring to boil, lower temperature to medium low, cover, and simmer for two hours. You may add seasoning to water. Make sure berries are always covered with water or they will dry out. After cooking, drain remaining water from wheat berries. Now they are ready to use in your favorite recipe or you may freeze them until you are ready to prepare your dish. When combining with rice, pasta, or beans, always precook the wheat berries. Like barley, wheat berries are very filling. L & B Kitchens offers a great wheat berry cookbook: (509) 337 8860.

Pasta

One of my favorite pastas to mix with rice is orzo. It is shaped like rice and easy to use in a variety of dishes. You may brown it with rice in a small amount of oil before adding liquid. It can be cooked right along with the rice. It requires less cooking time than rice, yet it does not tend to get mushy if cooked along with the rice.

Rice

I love to mix different kinds of rice (brown, white, and wild) together, or with beans, bulgar wheat, or pasta. Brown and wild rice require more cooking time, so you may need to precook some of the items if mixing. Most packages are quite clear with their cooking instructions.

Quinoa

Pronounced "Keen wa", this grain is very high in protein. It is difficult to find ... likely found in health food stores or co-ops. It looks like tiny pearls. You need to rinse it thoroughly before using. It is best when combined with other grains.

Kasha

Kasha, or cracked buckwheat is a great addition. Buckwheat is not a member of the wheat family. It is high in potassium and phosphorus, and it is gluten free. High in protein.

CHIPPED BEEF

When I call for chipped beef or dry pastrami in my recipes, I am referring to the 2.5 oz. packages found in your supermarket in the lunch meat section. It is often call Lean Beef, smoked, sliced, chopped, pressed, cooked. (Whew!) It is not to be confused with the beef that comes in a jar. One of the drawbacks of this product is the high sodium content. It also contains MSG. If you are sensitive to these additives, you may choose to use a low sodium, low fat, thin sliced ham. The same goes for Reuben in a Wrap. The pastrami which is packaged this way is much lower in fat than regular pastrami, which is great ... however again, if you are sensitive, choose an option.

FRUIT SWEETENERS

I have called for fruit sweetener or fruit juice concentrate in a number of my recipes. Fruit sweetener is sweeter than fruit juice concentrate. If you desire the sweetness of fruit sweetener yet you are unable to find the product, you may make your own with the following formula.

Formula

If a recipe calls for 1/2 cup fruit sweetener, use 1/2 cup frozen fruit juice concentrate (such as apple juice concentrate) plus half as much (1/4 cup) granulated fructose. (Granulated fructose is available at most grocery stores.)

If a recipe calls for 2/3 cup fruit sweetener, use 2/3 cup frozen fruit juice concentrate, plus 1/3 cup granulated fructose.

BE CAREFUL WHAT YOU PURCHASE
IF YOU HAVE DIETARY RESTRICTIONS.

According to the Rice Council in Houston, Texas, rice syrup is not a complex carbohydrate. Once it is changed into a syrup form, it becomes a simple carbohydrate, much like corn syrup. I have had many calls from people wanting to know if they may replace fruit sweetener with rice syrup in the recipes in the book. Rice syrup is less sweet than refined sugar (fructose is twice as sweet), so exchanging these items straight across would definitely change the sweetness of the end product. If rice syrup metabolizes like corn syrup, a person with dietary restrictions, (such as a person with high cholesterol, diabetes, high blood pressure) should consult his physician or dietitian before using such a product.

The analysis on each recipe in this book was done using fruit sweetener (peach, pear, pineapple juice) as the sweetening agent.

If you have any special dietary requirement, be sure to consult with your physician before using any recipe which contains special products such as those mentioned in this book.

DRESSINGS & SAUCES

CURRY DRESSING OR DIP

Great for vegetable dip or with crackers.

    1/3 cup non-fat mayonnaise
    2/3 cup non-fat yogurt
    1/2 - 1 tsp. curry powder
    1/4 tsp. cinnamon
    dash red pepper
    dash paprika

Combine above ingredients in small bowl. Refrigerate to blend flavors.

Makes 1 cup. 1 serving = 2 Tbsp.

11 calories	tr grams fat
1 grams carb.	1 mg cholesterol
1 grams protein	13 mg sodium

1 free food Exchange

FRENCH VINEGRETTE SALAD DRESSING

2/3 cup apple juice concentrate
1 Tbsp. tomato paste, low sodium
1/4 cup blackberry or raspberry vinegar
1/4 cup water
2 tsp. oil
salt (optional)
pepper
1 tsp. paprika

Combine of of the above ingredients in blender. Blend at medium high speed for 15 seconds.

Yield: 1 1/4 cup. 1 serving = 2 Tbsp.

40 calories	1 grams fat
8 grams carb.	0 mg cholesterol
tr grams protein	6 mg sodium

1/2 fruit Exchange

FRUIT DRESSING

This is great on Spring Spinach Salad.

> 2/3 cup orchard peach or other juice concentrate
> 1 Tbsp. Dijon mustard
> 1/3 cup raspberry vinegar
> 1/3 cup water
> 1/8 tsp. salt
> 2 Tbsp. oil
> 2 Tbsp. poppy seeds

Blend first five ingredients in blender for one minute.
Add oil slowly, blend a few more seconds. Add poppy seeds.

Yield: 2 cups. 1 serving = 2 Tbsp.

44 calories	2 grams fat
6 grams carb.	0 mg cholesterol
tr grams protein	32 mg sodium

1/3 fruit Exchange
1/2 fat Exchange

GREEK DRESSING OR DIP

I love Greek food. This dressing can be used in a variety
of ways. It is great on a Greek salad, as a dip for raw
vegetables, or a sauce on gyros.

> 1 1/2 cups non-fat plain yogurt
> 4 tsp. dry minced onion
> 2 tsp. dill weed
> 1 tsp. fresh or dry mint, chopped
> 1/2 cucumber, peeled, seeded, chopped fine

Combine all of the ingredients in a small bowl. Cover bowl
and refrigerate for two hours or more to combine flavors.
Fresh and tangy. Store in covered glass container in
refrigerator.

Yield: 1 3/4 cups. 1 serving = 2 Tbsp.

16 calories	0 grams fat
2 grams carb.	2 mg cholesterol
1 grams protein	16 mg sodium

1 free food Exchange

4

ITALIAN GARLIC DRESSING

This is a dressing I use often. I usually use only 2 tsp.
oil instead of the full 2 Tbsp. You may use your discretion.

> 1/3 cup apple juice concentrate
> 1/4 cup balsamic vinegar
> 1/2 cup water
> 2 Tbsp. oil
> 4 clove garlic, crushed
> 1/2 tsp. basil (fresh, if possible)
> 1/8 tsp. summer savory
> 1 tsp. minced chives
> dash pepper

Combine all ingredients in blender. Blend 20 seconds.
Store in glass container. Flavors blend as mixture sets.
Shake before serving.

Yield: 1 1/4 cups. 1 serving = 2 Tbsp.

40 calories	3 grams fat
4 grams carb.	0 mg cholesterol
tr grams protein	5 mg sodium

1/2 fat Exchange
1/3 fruit Exchange

MANGO SALAD DRESSING

    2 tsp. lemon juice
    1/3 cup rice vinegar (not sweetened)
    4 Tbsp. fruit sweetener or frozen juice concentrate
    2 Tbsp. Dijon mustard
    1 clove garlic, crushed
    2 Tbsp. oil
    1/3 cup water or unsalted chicken broth
    1/4 cup mango, chopped
    3 Tbsp. dried mango, chopped
    1/8 tsp. salt
    dash pepper

Combine all of the above ingredients in blender. Blend at medium speed for 2 minutes. This is a great dressing for spinach salad.

Makes 1 1/4 cups. 1 serving = 2 Tbsp.

46 calories	3 grams fat
5 grams carb.	0 mg cholesterol
tr grams protein	62 mg sodium

1 Fat Exchange

SPICY SWEET DIJON DRESSING

This dressing is nice with a fruit salad or fruit and greens mixed.

> 2/3 cup apple juice concentrate
> 1 Tbsp. Dijon mustard low sodium
> 1/4 cup raspberry vinegar
> 1/4 cup water
> 2 tsp. oil

Combine of of the above ingredients in blender. Blend at medium high speed for 15 seconds.

Yield: 1 1/4 cup. 1 serving = 2 Tbsp.

40 calories	1 grams fat
8 grams carb.	0 mg cholesterol
tr grams protein	25 mg sodium

1/2 fruit Exchange

MANGO TANGO CHUTNEY

A nice accompaniment with nearly any chicken dish.
Great in the summer with grilled chicken or kabobs.

> 1 ripe mango
> 1 ripe peach
> 2 Tbsp. green onion, chopped
> 2 Tbsp. raspberry vinegar
> 3 Tbsp. fruit sweetener (or frozen fruit juice
>   concentrate)
> 2 tsp. fresh mint (6-8 leaves)

Combine all ingredients in food processor. Blend 20-30
seconds. If you do not have a food processor, finely
chop all ingredients and mix together until blended.
Refrigerate.

1 serving = 2 Tbsp.

18 calories	0 grams fat
5 grams carb.	0 mg cholesterol
tr grams protein	tr mg sodium

1 free food Exchange

PAPAYA CHUTNEY

1 large papaya, peeled and chopped
1/2 cup red bell pepper, chopped fine
2 tsp. white wine vinegar or rice vinegar
2 Tbsp. fruit sweetener or frozen fruit juice
      concentrate
2 Tbsp. fresh mint, chopped
1 tsp. fresh ginger, grated

Combine all of the above ingredients in medium bowl.
Cover and refrigerate 1-2 hours.

1 serving = 2 Tbsp.

9 calories	tr grams fat
2 grams carb.	0 mg cholesterol
tr grams protein	tr mg sodium

1 free food Exchange

BARBECUE SAUCE

This is rather spicy. Enjoy!

> 1 15 oz. can low sodium tomato sauce
>   or tomato chunks in puree
> 2/3 cup water
> 2 Tbsp. dry minced onion
> 2 cloves garlic, minced
> 1/4 cup rice vinegar
> 1/4 cup fruit sweetener
> 2 Tbsp. Dijon mustard
> 1 tsp. Worchestershire
> 1/4 tsp. chili powder
> 1/2 tsp. cinnamon
> 1/2 tsp. ground cloves
> 1/4 tsp. paprika
> 2 drops liquid smoke

In medium saucepan, combine all ingredients. Cook five minutes over medium high heat, stirring constantly. When mixture begins to bubble, turn heat to low and simmer on stove for one hour. Let cool before using. Mixture thickens as it cools. Makes 2 cups.

1 serving = 2 Tbsp.

25 calories	tr grams fat
6 grams carb.	0 mg cholesterol
1 grams protein	68 mg sodium

1 vegetable Exchange

CAJUN SPICE SAUCE

This is the sauce I use in my Cajun Shrimp/Chicken (see the recipes). It is also a good marinade for the barbecue. If you use it for a marinade, save a portion of the sauce aside to use with vegetables over rice.

> 2 cups tomato puree with tomato pieces, no salt added
> 2 Tbsp. paprika
> 1 Tbsp. cinnamon
> 1 Tbsp. cloves
> 1 Tbsp. garlic powder or 3 cloves garlic, minced
> 1 Tbsp. onion powder
> 1 Tbsp. black pepper
> 2 tsp. cayenne pepper
> 1/2 tsp. thyme

Combine the above ingredients in large bowl. Stir well. If using to marinate meat, set aside a portion of sauce to brush on meat during and after cooking.

20 calories	tr grams fat
5 grams carb.	0 mg cholesterol
1 grams protein	8 mg sodium

1 free food Exchange

6 Tbsp. = 1 fruit Exchange

INDIA SAUCE

A spicy change of pace. Nice on chicken served with rice and crispy green salad.

>   2/3 cup fruit juice sweetened apricot or peach
>   preserves
>   3 Tbsp. raspberry vinegar
>   2/3 cup orange juice
>   1/4 cup water
>   1 tsp. garlic powder (or 2 cloves fresh crushed)
>   1/4 tsp. ginger
>   1/4 tsp. tumeric
>   1/4 tsp. cumin
>   dash black pepper

Combine all of the above ingredients in medium size bowl. Stir until well blended. Cover and refrigerate 1-2 hours.

1 serving = 2 Tbsp.

22 calories	0 grams fat
6 grams carb.	0 mg cholesterol
tr grams protein	tr mg sodium

1/3 fruit Exchange

INDIA MARINADE

This is a rather mild version of an Indian marinade. To make it a bit more spicy, increase the amount of cumin and cinnamon, then add a dash of cayenne. This is great on chicken or prawns.

  1/3 cup apricot or peach conserve
  3/4 cup orange juice
  1/4 cup water
  3 Tbsp. raspberry or currant vinegar
  1/4 tsp. cloves (ground)
  1/4 tsp. cumin
  1/4 tsp. cinnamon
  1/8 tsp. tumeric

Combine all of the above ingredients in bowl or blender. Whisk together or blend on medium approximately 30 seconds. Refrigerate until you desire to use. A nice addition if you can find it: 1/4 cup chopped dried mango (unsweetened), or golden raisins, or another interesting dried fruit. Many wonderful items such as dried bing cherries, dried cran-berries, some unsweetened and some sweetened with fructose, are available in many gourmet shops and grocery stores. In Seattle we are fortunate to have many wonderful markets and grocery stores filled with new and interesting specialty items. It makes cooking and eating lots more fun.

1 serving = 2 Tbsp.

16 calories	0 grams fat
4 grams carb.	0 mg cholesterol
0 grams protein	tr mg sodium

1 free food Exchange

TERIYAKI MARINADE

This is one of two teriyaki marinades. Each has its own unique flavor.

> 2/3 cup fruit juice sweetened orange or
>   orange/pineapple or apricot preserves
> 3 Tbsp. low sodium soy sauce
> 2/3 cup orange juice
> 3 Tbsp. water
> 1/2 tsp. garlic powder or 1-2 cloves fresh
>   crushed garlic
> 1/4 tsp. ginger or 1/2 tsp. grated fresh ginger

Combine the above ingredients in large bowl. If using the sauce to marinate meat, set aside a portion to brush onto the surface of the meat during and after cooking.

1 serving = 2 Tbsp.

25 calories	0 grams fat
6 grams carb.	0 mg cholesterol
tr grams protein	129 mg sodium

1/3 fruit Exchange

TERIYAKI MARINADE AND SAUCE II

When summer comes along and everyone is outdoors grilling, the air will be filled with a tantalizing aroma from this marinade.

> 1/3 cup orange pineapple preserves
> 3/4 cup orange juice
> 1/4 cup water
> 3 Tbsp. soy sauce (low sodium)
> 3 Tbsp. raspberry vinegar
>   (other fruit vinegars will work)
> 2 cloves garlic, crushed
> 2 tsp. ginger, fresh, grated

Combine all of the above ingredients in small bowl or blender. Whisk or blend at medium speed until well combined. Let set for 2 hours before using to help flavors meld.

When making sauces it is fun to try different flavors of conserves and vinegars. Most of the fruit sweetened conserves contain approximately the same number of calories per serving. Be sure to read labels carefully.

Always keep the marinade that you are going to brush on the grilling meat separate from the portion used to steep the meat. The portion used for soaking the raw meat or fish should be discarded after use.

1 serving = 2 Tbsp.

18 calories	0 grams fat
4 grams carb.	0 mg cholesterol
tr grams protein	129 mg sodium

1 free food Exchange

PEANUT SAUCE

There are many versions of peanut sauce. This one is reminiscent of one served by the Hilton at the China exhibit several years ago in Seattle. The original recipe called for 10 cloves of garlic, and even for me that was a bit much! (Smile)

> 3 cloves garlic, crushed
> 4 coriander leaves, optional (some people reeeally do not like coriander or cilantro, so be careful)
> 1/2 cup natural peanut butter
> 2 Tbsp. low sodium soy sauce
> 1/2 cup water
> 3 tsp. fruit sweetened or apple juice concentrate
> 2 tsp. rice vinegar, rice wine, or sherry
> 2 tsp. lime juice
> 1 drop hot chili oil

Mince garlic in food processor and add coriander, if desired. (My advice: if you are not familiar with coriander or cilantro, taste it before you add it.) Add remaining ingredients to processor and blend well. Best if mixture sets over night to blend flavors. You may use a blender if you do not have a food processor. Makes approximately 1 cup.

1 serving = 1/4 cup

98 calories
3 grams carb.
4 grams protein

8 grams fat
0 mg cholesterol
163 mg sodium

1 high fat meat Exchange

PEANUT SAUCE II

A different twist without the garlic. Great on pasta.

> 1/4 cup peanut butter
> 2/3 cup water
> 2 tsp. hot sweet mustard (fruit juice sweetened)
> 2 tsp. soy sauce (reduced sodium)
> 2 green onions, chopped
> 1 clove, crushed
> 1/2 tsp. cumin
> dash hot sesame oil (optional)

Combine all of the above ingredients in medium sauce pan. Cook over medium heat, stirring constantly. When well heated, pour over pasta or cooked chicken. This works well with pasta as a chilled pasta salad, also. If using sauce in pasta salad, add green onions as a garnish after sauce is mixed with pasta instead of including onions in sauce. *See pasta salads. Yield: 1 1/4 cup

1 serving = 1/4 cup

167 calories   12 grams fat
8 grams carb.   0 mg cholesterol
7 grams protein   360 mg sodium

1/2 fruit Exchange
1 high fat meat Exchange
1 fat Exchange

SEAFOOD SAUCE

This is spicy and light ... and, unlike nearly every seafood sauce out there, it contains no refined sugar.

        1 cup tomato herb, or tomato plus*
        2 tsp. Worchestershire
        1 Tbsp. horseradish
        2 tsp. blueberry or raspberry vinegar

Whisk all of the ingredients together in small bowl. This is great with prawns or fish. The end product tastes quite different depending upon which tomato product you use. Both are good.

1 serving = 2 Tbsp.

28 calories   0 grams fat
7 grams carb.   0 mg cholesterol
0 grams protein   83 mg sodium

1 vegetable Exchange

*Tomato herb is made by Wax Orchards.
Tomato plus is made by Lewis Harvey.

MARINARA SAUCE

I use tomato puree with tomato chunks in many sauces because it contains less sodium and no sugar. You may add water, broth, or red wine depending on your own taste. This way you have more control over sodium and calories. Good tip: cooking wine usually contains more sodium than regular wine, so you may wish to use a less expensive brand of regular wine rather than cooking wine.

     2 cloves garlic, crushed
     1 onion, chopped
     2 cans (15 oz.) tomato puree with chunks, unsalted
     2/3 cup water
     3 Tbsp. Burgundy
     1 1/2 tsp. basil (fresh, if you have it)
     1 tsp. oregano
     1 tsp. fennel
     1 Tbsp. parsley, chopped
     1/2 tsp. salt, pepper to taste

     (optional: 1 Tbsp. capers or peppercorns,
     1/4 cup sliced black olives, 1 cup mushrooms,
     sliced ... not included in exchanges)

In large saucepan, saute garlic and onion in 1 tsp. oil. When onion is transparent, add remaining ingredients. (optional ingredients add just before serving.) Simmer sauce for 45 minutes to 1 hour over medium low heat. If sauce becomes too thick, add water. If serving with meatballs, add them 20 minutes before serving and increase heat slightly. Serve over pasta, gnocchi, or dish of choice. Sprinkle with fresh Parmesan, if desired.

Yield: 5 cups. 1 serving = 1/4 cup

21 calories	tr grams fat
5 grams carb.	0 mg cholesterol
1 grams protein	62 mg sodium

1 Vegetable Exchange

HEALTHY CREAM SAUCE

I use this sauce in recipes in place of a typical white sauce. It has very little fat and can be made using broth and no dairy products, if desired.

        2 tsp. margarine
        2 Tbsp. flour
        2 cups chicken or beef broth (unsalted)
        1/4 cup skim milk (or broth, if desired)
        2-3 Tbsp. instant potato flakes

In medium saucepan, melt margarine. Stir in flour until well blended. Remove from heat. Very slowly, add broth, a few spoonfuls at a time, stirring until smooth after each addition. Once sauce is smooth, add remaining broth and milk. Return sauce to medium heat and thicken to desired consistency with potato flakes. Salt and pepper to taste. Yield: 2 1/2 cups

1 serving = 1/4 cup

18 calories   tr grams fat
2 grams carb.   tr mg cholesterol
tr grams protein   13 mg sodium

1 free food Exchange

FRENCH TARRAGON SAUCE:
Add 1 1/2 tsp. chopped tarragon to healthy cream sauce.

CREAMY CAPER SAUCE

A tasty sauce to serve with fish, chicken, or beef.

1 tsp. oil
1 Tbsp. dehydrated minced onion
2 cloves garlic, crushed
3-4 Tbsp. flour
1 2/3 chicken broth, low sodium
2 Tbsp. white wine
1 Tbsp. Dijon mustard
2 tsp. capers

In large saucepan, saute onion and garlic in oil. Add flour, blending well. Remove from heat and add 1/4 cup chicken broth, stirring constantly until smooth. Slowly, add remaining broth a little at a time. Return pan to medium heat and stir until sauce becomes thick and bubbles. Blend in remaining ingredients. If thicker sauce is desired, thicken with instant potato flakes. Salt and pepper to your desired taste.

Yield: 9 servings. 1 serving = 3 Tbsp.

21 calories
3 grams carb.
tr grams protein

1 grams fat
0 mg cholesterol
31 mg sodium

1 free food Exchange

DIJON SAUCE

This is used in my Dijon chicken recipe

1 tsp. oil
4 clove garlic, crushed
3 Tbsp. flour
1 1/2 cups broth, unsalted
1/2 cup non-fat milk
2 Tbsp. Dijon mustard
1/8 tsp. salt

In large saucepan, saute garlic in oil. Add flour, blending well. Remove from heat and add 1/4 cup chicken broth, stirring constantly until smooth. Slowly, add remaining broth a little at a time. Return pan to medium heat and stir until sauce becomes thick and bubbles. Blend in remaining ingredients. If thicker sauce is desired, thicken with instant potato flakes. Salt and pepper to your desired taste.

Yield: 2 cups. 8 servings. 1 serving = 4 Tbsp.

25 calories
3 grams carb.
1 grams protein

1 grams fat
tr mg cholesterol
91 mg sodium

1 free food Exchange

MUSHROOM GRAVY

It was a great find when I discovered this flavorful idea. A nice addition to turkey day.

2 tsp. oil
1/4 cup onion, chopped
4 mushrooms, sliced
2 cloves garlic, crushed
3 Tbsp. flour
small amount water
2 cups beef bouillon, unsalted
1/4 cup red wine
thicken with instant potatoes, if necessary
1/8 tsp. salt
pepper to taste
2 cups sliced mushrooms

In large skillet, saute onions and mushrooms in hot oil. When both turn golden, add flour and stir until smooth. Remove mixture from heat and, very slowly, add bouillon and wine. Thicken with potato flakes, if desired. Add salt, pepper, and mushrooms. Stir until smooth. Serve hot. For Stroganoff, add 1/2 cup non-fat plain yogurt, just before serving.

Yield: 2 1/2 cups 10 servings. 1 serving = 1/4 cup

25 calories
6 grams carb.
1 grams protein

2 grams fat
0 mg cholesterol
45 mg sodium

1 free food Exchange
1/2 fat Exchange

BEEF MUSHROOM GRAVY

This tastes fattening, but it is not. (Heaven!)
It is a nice low-fat way to add a tasty sauce to a meal.

1 tsp. butter or margarine
1/4 cup minced onion
4 cloves garlic, crushed
3-4 large mushrooms, sliced
3 Tbsp. flour
2 1/4 cups beef broth, unsalted
3 Tbsp. red wine
3 Tbsp. tomato puree
1 tsp. Worchestershire sauce (low sodium)
salt and pepper to taste (optional)

In large skillet, melt butter or margarine. I use butter
to enhance the flavor since it is such a small amount. Add
garlic, onion, mushrooms, and cook until golden. Add flour,
cooking slightly. Remove from heat and add 1/4 cup of broth,
stirring constantly until mixture is smooth. Slowly, add
broth, a little at a time. When mixture is smooth, return
to heat and continue to cook until sauce thickens. (keep
stirring) Add remaining ingredients, simmer a few minutes,
and serve. Thicken with instant potatoes, if desired.
Additional tasty options: 5-6 sliced mushrooms and 2 tsp.
capers or peppercorns.

Makes 2 1/2 cups. 1 serving = 1/4 cup

10 calories	tr grams fat
3 grams carb.	tr mg cholesterol
1 grams protein	11 mg sodium

1 free food Exchange

CARAMEL DRIZZLE

Cook this slowly so it does not curdle.

> 3/4 cup fruit sweetener
> 1/2 cup regular evaporated milk
> 1 tsp. vanilla

Pour fruit sweetener into small saucepan, cook over medium heat, stirring constantly until mixture begins to bubble. Reduce heat and add milk, continuing to cook over medium low heat for five minutes. Add vanilla and remove from heat. Let cool slightly before serving.

Yield: 1 cup (16 servings). 1 serving = 1 Tbsp.

40 calories	tr grams fat
8 grams carb.	tr mg cholesterol
tr grams protein	8 mg sodium

1/2 fruit Exchange

CHOCOLATE DRIZZLE

This is good to drizzle over cakes or brownies.

    2 1/2 Tbsp. cocoa (imported Dutch works best)
    1 cup fruit sweetener
    3 Tbsp. non-fat evaporated milk
    1 tsp. vanilla

Combine cocoa and sweetener in small saucepan over medium
high heat. Bring to boil, stirring constantly. Turn down
heat, simmer for 5 minutes. Stir in milk and simmer 2
minutes. Add vanilla. Remove from heat and serve. Cool
before putting in container for storage. Keep refrigerated.

Yield: 1 1/4 cup. 1 serving = 1 Tbsp.
sauce (20 servings).

35 calories   tr grams fat
9 grams carb.   tr mg cholesterol
tr grams protein   3 mg sodium

1/2 fruit Exchange

26

KIWI MANGO DESSERT SAUCE

My son, Ron, is creative at so many things! This he made for his sweet Colleen.

      1 large mango, peeled, sliced
      3 kiwi, peeled and sliced
      1/2 cup banana/pineapple juice concentrate
      4 Tbsp. water

Prepare fruit and set aside. In medium bowl, mix together juice concentrate and water. Pour over fruit and marinate for 1 hour or more. Serve over non-fat frozen yogurt or other dessert.

Yield: 2 cups. 1 serving = 1/4 cup.

64 calories   tr grams fat
15 grams carb.   0 mg cholesterol
tr grams protein   6 mg sodium

1 fruit Exchange

LEMON SYRUP

I use this on German Pancakes, yet it works well with other goodies too.

1/4 cup lemon juice
1/4 cup fruit sweetener

1 serving = 2 Tbsp.

42 calories	0 grams fat
11 grams carb.	0 mg cholesterol
0 grams protein	0 mg sodium

2/3 fruit Exchange

LEMON FILLING / SPREAD

I use this in place of lemon curd on crumpets. Real
lemon curd is full of butter and eggs, so this can't
be called curd. It tastes great as a cake filling, too.

> 3 Tbsp. water
> 2 Tbsp. corn starch
> 1/2 cup fruit sweetener
> 1/4 cup lemon juice zest of small lemon
> 1/4 tsp. margarine

In small saucepan, combine water and cornstarch. Stir
until smooth. Add fruit sweetener and cook over low heat
until mixture thickens. Add lemon juice and continue cooking
for 1 minute. Stir in zest and remove from heat.

Yield: 1 cup. 1 serving = 2 Tbsp.

50 calories	tr grams fat
12 grams carb.	0 mg cholesterol
tr grams protein	2 mg sodium

1 fruit Exchange

SOUPS

BASIC SOUP BROTH RECIPE

Two dear friends, Debbie and Wanda, told me about this type of broth. This is my version. You may add your own goodies to make your favorite soup or chowder.

> 6 large white potatoes, (6 oz. each)
>   peeled and cut into 2" chunks
> 1 quart water
> 1 quart low sodium chicken broth
> 1 Tbsp. margarine or butter
> 1 cup non-fat milk

Spices: may vary depending on what chowder you are making. I usually use a salt free spice combination, such as Mrs. Dash's. There are many of these on the market or you can pick from your own spice rack.

In a stock-pot, boil potatoes until tender. When potatoes are done, pour liquid off into large bowl. Mash or whip potatoes until they are very smooth. Slowly, add 1 cup of liquid from bowl, continuing to mash potatoes as you add liquid. Blend in margarine and milk. Continue adding liquid until you have added a total of approximately four cups. This should produce approximately eight cups (2 quarts) of broth.

This is the broth used in several of the following soup recipes.

8 cups broth. 1 serving = 1 cup

135 calories	2 grams fat
27 grams carb.	tr mg cholesterol
3 grams protein	22 mg sodium

1 1/2 starch/bread Exchanges

BAKED POTATO SOUP

I first tasted this in a restaurant in Indianapolis.
Chris, the friend I was with, suggested I try to do
a low-fat version. This one's for you, Chris!

> 2 large baking potatoes, baked and cooled
> 1 recipe basic soup broth
> 1 tsp. oil
> 1 medium onion, finely chopped
> 2 cloves garlic, minced
> 2 slices (2 oz. total) Canadian bacon
> salt, and fresh ground pepper to taste
> 1 tsp. dill, optional
> finely chopped scallions, or chives.
> 1/3 cup fresh Parmesan, shredded

Leaving skin on, chop baked potatoes in 1/2" squares.
Add to prepared broth. In large skillet, heat oil over
medium high heat and saute onion and garlic for 3-5 minutes.
Add finely chopped bacon and cook together for several
minutes. Add this mixture to broth. Blend in spices, heat
well, and serve. Garnish with scallions and Parmesan cheese.

Makes 6-8 servings. 1 serving = 1 1/2 cup

218 calories	4 grams fat
38 grams carb.	8 mg cholesterol
8 grams protein	187 mg sodium

2 1/2 starch/bread Exchanges
1 fat Exchange

CREAMY FRENCH VEGETABLE SOUP

This is one of my favorite soups. It has a rather unusual ingredient ... a parsnip. Strange as it sounds this little veggie adds a sweet subtle flavor that can't be duplicated. I think it's what makes the soup! If you really don't like parsnips, you may delete it, but do try it at least once.

        2 tsp. oil
        1 tsp. butter
        2 shallots, chopped
        1 large onion, chopped
        2 large potatoes, (6 oz.) peeled and chopped
        6 large carrots, peeled and chopped
        1 large parsnip, peeled and chopped
        1 1/2 quarts low sodium chicken broth
        1/2 tsp. thyme
        dash marjoram
        1/4 tsp. salt

In large saucepan or stock-pot, over medium heat, combine oil and butter. Add shallots and onion. Saute until onion is soft and transparent. Add remaining vegetables and saute for an additional 3 minutes. Add broth and spices. Bring mixture to boil. Reduce heat to medium low and cover. Simmer 30-40 minutes, or until vegetables are soft. Turn off heat. Let soup set for 30 minutes to cool. Puree mixture in blender and return it to pan. The creamy texture is due to the pureed veggies. Serve with a dollop of non-fat yogurt cheese and parsley.

Makes 8 servings. 1 serving= 1 1/4 cup.

93 calories	2 grams fat
18 grams carb.	tr mg cholesterol
2 grams protein	84 mg sodium

1 starch/bread Exchange
1 vegetable Exchange

LENTIL SOUP

This is a very hearty soup. You can vary the spices to your taste. Great on a cold wintry day with hot sour dough bread.

 1 tsp. oil
 1 large onion, chopped
 2 cloves garlic, crushed
 1 stalk celery, chopped
 2 carrots, chopped
 2 cup lentils, rinsed and drained
 2 quarts water
 1/2 cup lean smoked ham, chopped
 1 tsp. cumin
 1/2 tsp. mint
 1/4 tsp. oregano
 1/4 tsp. salt, pepper to taste

In large skillet, saute onion and garlic in oil. When transparent, add celery and carrots and saute an additional 3 minutes. In large stock-pot, combine vegetables with remaining ingredients, except spices. Bring mixture to boil, reduce heat and simmer soup with lid on for 1 hour. Add spices, salt, and pepper to taste. Serve with dollop of yogurt sprinkled lightly with dill weed or mint, if desired.

Makes 6 servings. 1 serving = 1 1/4 cup.

197 calories	2 grams fat
32 grams carb.	5 mg cholesterol
15 grams protein	220 mg sodium

2 starch/bread Exchanges
1 low-fat meat Exchange

OREGON COAST CHOWDER

This can be made with fresh or canned clams. A favorite in restaurants throughout the Northwest where clam digging is a great pastime.

    1 recipe basic soup broth
    2 - 6 oz. cans minced clams
    1 bay leaf
    2 cloves garlic, minced
    1/2 tsp. salt, and pepper to taste
    2 slices Canadian bacon, finely chopped (2 oz.)
    1 tsp. oil
    1 large onion, finely chopped
    1 1/2 cups celery, finely chopped
    2 cups finely diced potatoes
    1/2 cup green pepper, finely chopped, (optional)
    oyster crackers

In large stock pot, make basic soup broth. Add clams (drain clams only if desired). Add bay leaf, spices, and Canadian bacon to broth and simmer over medium heat. In large skillet, saute onion, celery, and potatoes in oil until potatoes are somewhat cooked. Add sauted vegetables to broth. Add green pepper, if desired. Top servings with oyster crackers and chopped chives. (6 oyster crackers per bowl)

Makes 8 servings. Serving = 1 1/2 cup.

230 calories	4 grams fat
41 grams carb.	31 mg cholesterol
10 grams protein	317 mg sodium

2 1/2 starch/bread Exchanges
1 fat Exchange

MINESTRONE SOUP

You may have already discovered that I do not
like to over-cook vegetables! Even in soups. I
prefer to simmer the broth with the spices to
enrich the flavor, but everything tastes fresher
when the vegetables are not cooked to mush.

2 quarts low sodium beef broth
1/3 fresh chopped basil (or 2 tsp. dried basil)
1/2 tsp. sage
2-3 cloves garlic, put through press or minced
1/4 cup Burgundy wine
1 cup kidney beans, cooked (low sodium, if canned)
1 tsp. oil
4 slices Canadian bacon, finely chopped
1 large onion, chopped
1 potato, finely chopped
2/3 cup celery, finely chopped
3 tomatoes, peeled, seeded, chopped
2 carrots, chopped
1 zucchini, chopped
1 cup fresh spinach, finely chopped
1 cup pasta
1/2 tsp. salt and pepper to taste
fresh Parmesan (2 Tbsp.)

In large stock-pot, combine first six ingredients. Simmer
over medium heat while preparing other ingredients. In
large skillet, heat oil over medium high heat and saute
bacon, onion, potato, and celery for 5-7 minutes. Add this
mixture to broth and continue to simmer. Approximately 15
minutes before serving soup, add remaining vegetables and
pasta. Simmer until vegetables are done, but crisp. Salt
and pepper to taste. Top individual servings with parsley
and Parmesan.

Makes 10 servings. 1 serving = 1 1/2 cup.

123 calories
20 grams carb.
6 grams protein

2 grams fat
4 mg cholesterol
233 mg sodium

1 starch/bread Exchange
1 vegetable Exchange

SALMON CHOWDER

This is a great dish in the Northwest where fresh salmon is abundant. Great with leftover grilled salmon. Point of interest: red sockeye salmon has stronger flavor, but is slightly higher in fat than the pink or silver salmon.

    1 recipe basic soup broth
    1 tsp. oil
    1 large onion, finely chopped (Walla Walla sweet
          is great if it is in season.)
    1 cup finely chopped celery
    1 cup skinless boneless pink salmon (4 oz.)
    1 tsp. dill weed
    1/2 tsp. thyme
    1/2 tsp. salt and fresh ground pepper to taste

Make broth in large stock-pot and keep warm. In large skillet, heat oil and saute onion and celery until transparent. (If you wish to add a 1/4 tsp. of butter, this will enhance flavors.) Stir in salmon and spices. Pour this entire mixture into broth. Serve with hot sour dough bread and fresh green salad. Top soup with small amount of fresh shredded Parmesan or low-fat cheddar.

Makes 6-8 servings. 1 serving = 1 1/2 cups.

167 calories   3 grams fat
30 grams carb.   8 mg cholesterol
6 grams protein   178 mg sodium

2 starch/bread Exchanges
1 fat Exchange

SALADS~SNACKS

CHOPPED SALAD

This is my rendition of a very FAVORITE which is served at one of my favorite restaurants: PALOMINO! It can also be found at Cucina Cucina ... but you must visit Washington to find these charming spots.

> 1 head Romaine lettuce, finely chopped
> 1/2 cup red onion, finely chopped (optional)
> 1 cup celery, finely chopped
> 1 cup tomato, seeded, and finely chopped
> 1 cup fresh or frozen baby peas
> 3 Tbsp. Canadian bacon, finely chopped
> 4 leaves fresh basil, finely chopped
> 1/2 cup toasted almonds, (optional)

Have you figured out why they call it chopped salad?

Dressing: 1/2 cup fat free mayonnaise
1/2 cup non-fat plain yogurt
1 Tbsp. fruit sweetener or apple juice concentrate
2 tsp. rice vinegar
1/4 tsp. garlic powder
1/4 tsp. salt
white pepper to taste

In large bowl, combine all salad ingredients. Mix dressing in blender. Pour over salad and mix well.

Yield: 8 servings. 1 serving = approx. 1 cup

98 calories	5 grams fat
9 grams carb.	4 mg cholesterol
5 grams protein	135 mg sodium

2 vegetable Exchanges
1 fat Exchange

GARDEN SALAD

As bright and colorful as a sunny summer day. This is
another "GOOD FOR YOU" salad. Inspired by Myrna Benskir
recipe.

> 1/2 cup Canadian bacon, finely chopped
> 2 cups broccoli flowerets
> 1 cup cauliflower, chopped
> 1/2 cup red onion, chopped
> 1/2 cup golden raisins
> 1/4 cup dry roasted sunflower seeds

Dressing: 2/3 cup non-fat mayonnaise
> 1/3 cup non-fat plain yogurt
> 2 Tbsp. vinegar
> 3 Tbsp. apple juice concentrate

In small skillet, saute bacon until crisp. Pat out as
much oil as possible with paper towel. In large salad
bowl, combine all of the ingredients except sunflower
seeds. In small bowl, whisk together dressing ingredients
until well blended. Pour over salad and refrigerate
2 hours. Add sunflower seeds just before serving.

Yield: 10 servings. 1 serving = 1/2 cup

80 calories	3 grams fat
12 grams carb.	4 mg cholesterol
4 grams protein	98 mg sodium

1 vegetable Exchange
1/2 fat Exchange
1/2 fruit Exchange

GREEK SALAD

This is another "meal in itself salad" for lunch, or great with cold chicken. Wonderful on a warm summer evening with hot homemade pita bread or sourdough rolls.

> 1 large bunch spinach, washed, chopped
> 1 cucumber, (regular or English) peeled, seeded, chopped
> 8 cherry tomatoes, seeded and quartered
> 1/4 red onion, sliced
> 1/3 cup feta cheese, crumbled
> 8 - 10 Greek olives, seeded, sliced
> 3 cloves roasted garlic (optional)

Combine the above ingredients in large salad bowl. If preparing ahead of time, do not add cheese, olives, or garlic. Add these items just before serving. Use dressing of choice or Greek yogurt dressing.

Yield: 4 servings. 1 serving = 1/4 of salad

73 calories	4 grams fat
8 grams carb.	8 mg cholesterol
4 grams protein	247 mg sodium

1 vegetable Exchange
1 fat Exchange

MORNING GLORY SALAD

This is very pretty and can be made with a variety of fruits depending on what is in season. In the winter, mandarin oranges will brighten it up. I have listed options for each ingredient ... you make the choice.

Nutrition information based on first choice.

> 4 small heads of Belgian endive
> 12 strawberries, sliced
>> or 2 large apples, thinly sliced
> 4 mandarin oranges, sectioned
>> or 2 oranges sliced in halves
> 2 kiwi fruit, peeled, sliced
> 3/4 cup blueberries
>> or 1/2 cup sliced red grapes (20)

On large platter, arrange endive leaves on outer edge as flower petals. Layer each fruit in order in a circle, overlapping slightly if necessary. Work your way to the center with strawberries on outside, followed by oranges, then kiwi, with the center being a solid circle of blueberries or grape slices. Your salad should be circles of color with endive petals on outside.

Yield: 8 servings. 1 serving = approx. 3/4 cup

43 calories   tr grams fat
10 grams carb.   0 mg cholesterol
1 grams protein   8 mg sodium

2/3 fruit Exchange

PASTA LIGHT SALAD

This is a light version of a salad that originally
contained lots of oil and cheese. This one has more
crunchies and less fat.

    1 - 8 oz. pkg. Rotini pasta, cooked and cooled
    1 1/4 cup reduced calorie Italian dressing
            with cheese
    1 cup celery, finely chopped
    1 large jar chopped artichoke hearts
            (packed in water)
    1/2 English cucumber, peeled, seeded, chopped
    1/2 golden bell pepper, chopped
    1/2 red bell pepper, chopped
    1/2 cup sliced black olives, (approx. 12)
    1/4 cup shredded fresh Parmesan (optional)

In large salad bowl, combine pasta, dressing, celery,
and artichoke hearts. Refrigerate 1-2 hours. Just before
serving, add remaining ingredients and mix together well.

Yield: 12 servings. 1 serving = approx. 2/3 cup

123 calories   4 grams fat
18 grams carb.   3 mg cholesterol
4 grams protein   297 mg sodium

1 starch/bread Exchange
1 fat Exchange

PEANUT THAI SALAD

I have included two other peanut sauces in this book.
I am adding a third: the dressing for this salad. You may
substitute one of the others if you prefer. You may also
use almonds in place of peanuts with an Italian dressing.

> 1/2 cabbage, finely shredded (1 - 16 oz. pkg.)
> 4 green onions, finely chopped
> 2 carrots, shredded
> 1 pkg. top ramin type noodles, crushed
> 3 Tbsp. peanuts, chopped

Dressing:
> 2 Tbsp. salad oil
> 3 Tbsp. rice vinegar
> 3 Tbsp. fruit sweetener or apple juice concentrate
> 2 Tbsp. peanut butter
> 2 tsp. low sodium soy sauce
> 1/4 cup water

In large bowl, combine first four ingredients. Set aside.
In blender, combine dressing ingredients. Pour over salad
and chill for 1 hour.

Yield: 6 cups. 1 serving = 2/3 cup of salad

114 calories   7 grams fat
11 grams carb.   0 mg cholesterol
3 grams protein   70 mg sodium

1 starch/bread Exchange
1 fat Exchange

SESAME CHICKEN SALAD

This can be made with a variety of salad dressings. I often use the mango dressing (see recipe) and add mandarin oranges to the salad. Here is the original.

> 2 single chicken breasts, grilled
>   (6 oz. cooked weight)
> 3 Tbsp. sesame seeds
> 1 head leaf or bibb lettuce, in bite size pieces
> 1 can water chestnuts, sliced, rinsed
> 1 cup snow peas (pea pods), sliced
> 6 green onions, sliced

I usually marinate the chicken breasts in teriyaki marinade the day I make the salad. Grill the chicken breasts, slice them, and sprinkle with sesame seeds. Wrap in foil to keep warm while preparing salad. In large salad bowl, combine lettuce, water chestnuts, snow peas, and onions. Toss with dressing (recipe below). Divide salad onto four plates and top each salad with one half of each chicken breast.

Yield: 4 servings. 1 serving = 1/4 of salad

Dressing: 2/3 cup orange Juice, 1 Tbsp. oil, 2 Tbsp. rice vinegar, 3 Tbsp. water, 1/4 tsp. fresh ginger, and 1/4 tsp. fresh garlic, crushed.

180 calories	9 grams fat
11 grams carb.	36 mg cholesterol
17 grams protein	37 mg sodium

2 low-fat meat Exchanges
1 vegetable Exchange
1 fat Exchange

SPRING SPINACH SALAD

This is a variation of a salad served by Carole McGavick
at one of her famous showers. I make this salad for every
occasion I possibly can!

> 1 large bunch fresh spinach, washed, chopped (6 cups)
> 12 large fresh strawberries, sliced
> 1 medium jicama, peeled and sliced in strips 1/4" x 2"
> 2 kiwi, peeled and sliced in half circle pieces
> 1 cup mandarin orange slices

Combine all of the above ingredients in a large glass
salad bowl. This salad is so gorgeous that it deserves
to be seen. Chill. When ready to serve, toss with fruit
dressing. (see recipe)

Yield: 4 large servings. 1 serving = 1/4 of salad

96 calories   1 grams fat
23 grams carb.   0 mg cholesterol
4 grams protein   100 mg sodium

1 vegetable Exchange
1 fruit Exchange

SUPER SALAD

The reason I call this super salad is that it is full of
color, crispness, and fiber. It contains twice the fiber
per serving as a salad made with head lettuce, tomato,
radish, onion, and mushroom. It is also great for re-runs
as the ingredients don't tend to get soggy.

  1/2 head of shredded or chopped cabbage (3 cups)
  1 cup chopped carrots
  1 cup chopped broccoli
  1 large red pepper, chopped
  1 cup chopped parsley

Combine the above ingredients in a large salad bowl. Top
with your favorite dressing. This salad is very nutritious,
low calorie, and filling.

Yield: 6 servings. 1 serving = 3/4 cup

22 calories	tr grams fat
5 grams carb.	8 mg cholesterol
1 grams protein	177 mg sodium

1 vegetable Exchange

TACO SALAD

This is easy to prepare. The ingredients can be altered to your own tastes. I love to add green chilies to the refried beans.

1 head leaf or bibb lettuce, chopped
1 tomato, seeded, and chopped
1 cup celery, chopped
1 cup bean sprouts
1 onion, chopped
1/3 lb. extra lean ground beef
1/2 tsp. chili powder
1/2 tsp. cumin
1/4 tsp. cinnamon
1/2 tsp. garlic powder
1 can vegetarian style refried beans (16 oz.)
1 small can diced green chilies (4 oz.)
1/2 cup low-fat cheddar cheese (or jack), shredded
10 black olives, sliced
20 fat free corn tortilla chips (2 oz.)

In a large salad bowl, combine first four ingredients. (If preparing ahead, add tomatoes when ready to serve.) Refrigerate. In large skillet, saute onion in 1 tsp. oil. Add ground beef and brown well. Stir in spices. (Refried beans & chilies may be added to ground beef or heated and layered over beef on salad) Make small well in center of salad mixture. Layer beef, beans, and chilies in this well. Garnish with shredded cheese, olives, and chips.

4 dinner size servings. 1 serving = 1/4 of salad

314 calories   11 grams fat
38 grams carb.   31 mg cholesterol
22 grams protein   814 mg sodium

2 starch/bread Exchanges
1 vegetable Exchange
2 low-fat meat Exchanges
1 fat Exchange

TARRAGON CHICKEN SALAD

I love this kind of salad. This one was inspired by Emily and Peggy, two talented artists from Bainbridge Island, Washington. Creative artists are often creative cooks!

> 3 single chicken breasts (12 oz. cooked weight)
>   cooked, cooled, shredded
> 1 cup celery, sliced
> 2 golden delicious apples, chopped
> 1 can sliced water chestnuts
> 1 cup red seedless grapes, halved
> 1/2 cup toasted chopped pecans (or almonds)
> 1 cup non-fat plain yogurt
> 1/4 cup non-fat mayonnaise
> 1 Tbsp. chopped tarragon (fresh, if possible)
> 1/8 tsp. salt
> pepper to taste

In large salad bowl, combine chicken, celery, apples, water chestnuts, grapes, and pecans. In small bowl, whisk remaining ingredients together for dressing. Pour over salad and toss well. Refrigerate for two hours to blend flavors. Serve with hot sour dough rolls.

Yield: 4 large dinner size servings. 1 serving = 1/4 of salad (If serving with entree, salad serves 10)

314 calories	10 grams fat
27 grams carb.	71 mg cholesterol
30 grams protein	170 mg sodium

3 low-fat meat Exchanges
2 fruit Exchanges
1 fat Exchange

CHUTNEY MINI MEATBALLS

A simple nummy pupu from Vy's Kula Kane collection.
I have changed it a bit to lower fat content.

>   1/2 lb. ground turkey breast
>   1/2 lb. extra lean ground beef
>   1/3 cup peach, mango, or apricot chutney
>   fruit sweetened
>   1/3 cup matzo meal or bread crumbs
>   1/2 tsp. garlic powder
>   1/8 tsp. pepper

In large bowl, combine turkey and beef. Work with fork
or your fingers to combine meats well. With fork, stir
in remaining ingredients. When blended, shape into small
meatballs. Brown well on all sides in skillet which has
been sprayed with non-stick coating. Option: place on foil
and cook in covered outdoor barbecue grill. Cooking time
on grill approx. 10-12 minutes. (Turn to cook evenly.)

Makes 48 mini meatballs. 1 serving = 3 meatballs.

53 calories	2 grams fat
4 grams carb.	14 mg cholesterol
6 grams protein	28 mg sodium

1 low-fat Meat Exchange

CRANBERRY CRACKER SPREAD

This is a recipe from Betsy Sestrap. It is so easy and so tasty. You can make it a variety of ways; this is one of my favorites at holiday times.

> 1 - 8 oz. package fat free cream cheese
>   softened slightly
> 1 cup cranberry chutney, fruit juice sweetened*
>   (or your favorite flavor chutney)

In center of serving platter, mound cream cheese into ball with top flattened slightly. Pour chutney on top of cream cheese. Serve with water crackers.

Makes 48 snacks. 1 serving = 1/4 oz. cheese/chutney

13 calories	0 grams fat
2 grams carb.	1 mg cholesterol
1 grams protein	28 mg sodium

1 free food Exchange

49

MUSHROOMS STUFFED

Simply delicious!

    1 lb. large firm mushrooms, cleaned
    1 tsp. oil
    1 Tbsp. dry minced onion
    6 oz. fat free cream cheese, softened
    3 Tbsp. fresh grated Parmesan cheese

Remove stems from mushrooms, set aside. Saute mushroom c
in 1 tsp. oil for 3 minutes. Remove caps and set on tray.
Mushrooms have a lot of water, so you may have to dry them
slightly with paper towel. Chop mushroom stems and saute
them in remaining oil and juice. Add minced onion and cook
until mixture is soft and golden. Remove mixture from heat.
Stir in cream cheese and Parmesan. Fill each mushroom with
small spoonful of mixture. Place mushrooms on heavy baking
sheet and broil until filling bubbles. Cool slightly before
serving.

Makes 18 filled mushrooms. 1 serving = 3 mushrooms.

70 calories	2 grams fat
5 grams carb.	7 mg cholesterol
7 grams protein	230 mg sodium

1 low-fat meat Exchange
+ 1 free food Exchange

BEEF IN BREAD DIP

I have had several versions of this recipe. Spinach can
be added, if desired. I like to use unsalted, hickory-
smoked, almonds for the nuts. It adds a great smoky taste.
Thank you to my dear friend, Vy Manning, for sharing your
Pupu recipes with me.

    1 large round loaf sour dough bread
    1 - 4 oz. package light cream cheese
    4 oz. fat free cream cheese
    2 Tbsp. skim milk
    3/4 cup non-fat plain yogurt
    1 - 2 1/2 oz. package dried beef
    2 Tbsp. minced dry onion
    2 Tbsp. chopped green pepper
    1/8 tsp. black pepper
    1/4 cup chopped pecans

Prepare a few hours ahead so flavor is enhanced. Slice top
off bread. Make crisscross in soft bread and remove. Cut in
cubes and store in plastic container. Combine all other
ingredients and mix together well. Fill hollow loaf with
dip. Cover with bread lid. Wrap in foil and refrigerate for
several hours. Dip bread cubes.

Makes 2 1/2 cups dip/10 servings. 1 serving = 3 Tbsp.
(dip only, without bread)

80 calories	5 grams fat
5 grams carb.	10 mg cholesterol
6 grams protein	240 mg sodium

1/2 non-fat milk Exchange
1 fat Exchange

VEGGIE STYLE SOUR DOUGH BREAD DIP

This is a low-fat version of a popular snack. A great way to sneak in some extra veggies. This can be a good onion dip, too if you substitute dry onion soup for veggie soup and leave out the extra onion. If you are watching sodium, read the labels ... you might want to eliminate some of the dry bouillon in the soup mix.

> 1 large loaf round sourdough bread
> 1 cup non-fat mayonnaise
> 1 1/4 cup plain non-fat yogurt
> 1 pkg. dry vegetable soup mix
> 1/2 cup finely chopped onion
> 1 tsp. dill weed
> 1 pkg. frozen chopped spinach, thawed, and
>   squeezed dry

Prepare a few hours ahead so flavor is enhanced. Slice top off bread. Make crisscross in soft bread and remove. Cut in cubes and store in plastic container. Combine all other ingredients and mix together well. Fill hollow loaf with dip. Cover with bread lid. Wrap in foil and refrigerate for several hours. Dip bread cubes. When cubes are devoured, cut additional cubes and tear pieces off loaf. You can eat dip as well as container.

16 servings:3 cups dip. 1 serving = 3 Tbsp.

Dip only:
24 calories	tr grams fat
4 grams carb.	tr mg cholesterol
2 grams protein	247 mg sodium

1 Vegetable Exchange

BEEF ROLL UPS

This is one of the recipes for the kids' cookbook. I think adults will enjoy it too, so I'm sharing it with you.

4 oz. non-fat cream cheese, softened
2 Tbsp. light cream cheese, softened
1 Tbsp. non-fat mayonnaise
2 Tbsp. finely chopped pecans
1/4 tsp. dill weed
1/4 tsp. garlic powder
1 - 2 1/2 oz. pkg. dried beef or pastrami

Using electric mixer, cream together first three ingredients. If too thick, add small amount of milk. Stir in nuts and spices. Divide spread evenly among pieces of dry beef. Spread mixture gently over each piece, being careful not to tear meat. Roll each piece up jelly roll fashion. Refrigerate for 1 hour. Slice into 1" slices if desired.

Yield: 9 full rolls. 1 serving = 1 roll

40 calories	2 grams fat
1 grams carb.	7 mg cholesterol
4 grams protein	190 mg sodium

1/2 med. fat meat Exchange

SPINACH ROLL UPS

This is a version of a great pupu from one of Debbie Lewallen's famous Christmas luncheons! The original recipe was from Danny Mathers.

    1 cup non-fat mayonnaise
    1 cup non-fat plain yogurt
    1 1/2 tsp. salt free lemon herb seasoning
        or a favorite salad dressing mix
    1 tsp. dill weed
    1 pkg. frozen chopped spinach, thawed, squeezed dry
    1/4 cup finely chopped dried beef
        (1 1/4 oz. or half package.)
    3/4 cup crab or shrimp meat. (canned, rinsed)
    12 flour tortillas

In large bowl, combine mayonnaise and spices. Mix well. Stir in spinach until well blended. Add dried beef and crab meat. Divide evenly and spread over the 12 tortillas. Roll each tortilla up jelly roll style. Place on large plate and cover tightly with foil or plastic. Refrigerate overnight. Slice in 1" slices to serve. Each tortilla = 6 slices.

Yield: 72 pieces. 1 serving = 3 pieces
(yield: 24 servings of 3 pieces each)

64 calories	1 grams fat
10 grams carb.	4 mg cholesterol
3 grams protein	87 mg sodium

1 starch/bread Exchange

POPCORN & CHEESE

Very easy snack!

    6 cups popped, popcorn*
    1/3 cup fresh grated Parmesan

Pop corn in blow popper. (This adds no oil.) Remove any unpopped seeds. Place popcorn in large glass bowl. Sprinkle with Parmesan. (Do not mix cheese into popcorn) Microwave on high for 1-1 1/2 minutes. (test with your own microwave, as they are all different!) Remove from microwave and stir with fork. (Some of the Parmesan will have melted down into mixture.) Stir to evenly distribute cheese.

Makes 6 cups. 1 serving = 1 cup

50 calories	2 grams fat
5 grams carb.	4 mg cholesterol
3 grams protein	102 mg sodium

1/2 starch/bread Exchange
1/2 fat Exchange

SNACKER CRACKERS

These are easy to prepare, low calorie, and tasty.
Bet you can't eat just TEN!

> 5 cups oyster crackers
> 1 tsp. Canola oil
> 1 tsp. dry minced onion
> 1 tsp. garlic powder
> 1 tsp. onion powder
> 2 tsp. dry dill weed
> 1 tsp. dry parsley flakes
> 2 tsp. water
> 1/3 cup non-fat yogurt
> 1/3 cup fresh shredded Parmesan

Measure crackers into 9" x 13" baking dish; set aside.
In large Teflon coated skillet, heat oil to medium heat.
Add dry onion and stir rapidly with wooden spoon. Quickly,
add other spices, stirring constantly. Add water; mix well.
Stir in yogurt until well blended. Add oyster crackers and
stir mixture until spices coat crackers. Spoon entire
mixture back into cake pan. Sprinkle Parmesan evenly over
crackers. Bake at 275 degrees for 6-8 minutes, stirring
occasionally. Bake until Parmesan is melted. Cool crackers
thoroughly and place them in covered container for storage.

1 serving = 1/2 cup

127 calories   5 grams fat
18 grams carb.   3 mg cholesterol
4 grams protein   362 mg sodium

1 starch/bread Exchange
1 fat Exchange

BREADS & JAMS

GERMAN PANCAKES

As a child I was a picky eater and would not eat a pancake unless it looked like Mickey Mouse! However, my Aunt Eve made these special pancakes and I have loved them forever!! My regular version has no cream and it's a bit lighter than the real thing. I have done a light version for those watching cholesterol.

Would this work for the ingredients?
        1 cup flour
        1 cup skim milk
        2 Tbsp. fruit sweetener
        4 eggs *
        dash nutmeg

        * For light version use 4 egg whites plus 1 egg instead of 4 eggs.

In large bowl, measure flour. In smaller bowl, combine remaining ingredients, beating well. Slowly, add egg mixture to flour mixture, beating with whisk until well blended. Set aside. Heat griddle or Teflon coated skillet to medium high. Brush skillet with 1/4 tsp. oil. Using ladle, scoop approx. 1/2 cup of batter on to hot skillet. Cook until set and bubbly, then turn over for 10-15 seconds. Best when eaten immediately. Serve with lemon syrup.

1 serving = 1 pancake. Yield: 6 large cakes.

Regular version:
147 calories   4 grams fat
20 grams carb.   143 mg cholesterol
8 grams protein   63 mg sodium

1 starch/bread Exchange
1 med. fat meat Exchange

Light version:
120 calories   1 grams fat
20 grams carb.   36 mg cholesterol
7 grams protein   63 mg sodium

1 starch/bread Exchange
1 low-fat meat Exchange

LONDON CAKES

A breakfast pancake, this is an adaptation of a recipe from JRB, a true "Artiste". It is interesting how many artists create incredible edible art, but then food is just another art form! Again, I have tried to lower the fat content considerably.

This batter is best when made the night before and refrigerated overnight.

　　　1 Tbsp. yeast
　　　1/4 tsp. water
　　　2 Tsp. oil
　　　1 1/2 cup skim milk
　　　1/3 cup low-fat ricotta cheese
　　　2 cups flour

Combine first four ingredients in small saucepan. Stir over low heat until mixture is just warm and yeast is dissolved. Stir in ricotta. When blended, slowly add flour, 1/2 cup at a time, stirring until smooth. Pour into a container and cover. Refrigerate over night or let set 30 minutes. Cook on hot griddle which has been sprayed with non-stick coating.

Yield: 8 pancakes. 1 serving = 1 pancake

177 calories   5 grams fat
27 grams carb.   4 mg cholesterol
6 grams protein   105 mg sodium

1 starch/bread Exchange
1 fat Exchange

SCONES

Scones have always been a big tradition in the State of Washington. (okay, maybe not as big as ESPRESSO) I did not grow up here, yet I enjoy the State Fair and the scones.

2 cups flour
1 tsp. baking powder
1/2 tsp. baking soda
1/8 tsp. salt
3-4 Tbsp. fruit sweetener or frozen juice concentrate
2 Tbsp. oil
1/2 cup non-fat yogurt
1 egg white
2 tsp. vanilla
1/4 cup currants or dried cranberries

In a large bowl, combine dry ingredients, blending well. Add fruit sweetener and oil. Stir together until mixture resembles coarse crumbs. In separate bowl, whisk together yogurt, egg white, and vanilla. Using fork, stir liquid into dry mixture. (If mixture is dry, add a bit of water.) Add currants. On floured board, knead dough several times until smooth. Pat dough into 8-10" circle on baking sheet, which has been sprayed with non-stick spray. Lightly mark circle into 10 wedges. Bake 10-15 minutes, until just golden, at 400 degrees.

Cut into 10 servings. 1 serving = 1 wedge

150 calories   3 grams fat
26 grams carb.   1 mg cholesterol
4 grams protein   109 mg sodium

1 starch/bread Exchange
1/2 fruit Exchange
1 fat Exchange

GRANOLA SCONES

This is the best of all world's breakfast in my opinion.
It is quick to fix, hot, cozy, and healthy. It's so good
it could be considered one of my comfort foods.

1 1/2 cup flour
1 tsp. baking powder
1/2 tsp. baking soda
1 cup low-fat, fruit juice sweetened granola
1/3 cup fruit sweetener
2 Tbsp. oil
1 egg white
1/2 cup non-fat plain yogurt
2 Tbsp. skim milk
1/4 cup chopped dates, (optional)

Combine first four ingredients and blend well. In separate
bowl, combine fruit sweetener, oil, yogurt, and egg white.
Beat well and add to flour mixture. Add enough milk to mal
mixture doughy, but not sticky. On floured board or cloth,
knead dough until smooth. Transfer to baking sheet which h
been sprayed with non stick coating. Bake 10-15 minutes at
375 degrees or until golden.

Cut into 10 wedges. 1 serving = 1 wedge
163 calories   4 grams fat
27 grams carb.   0 mg cholesterol
5 grams protein   93 mg sodium

1 starch/bread Exchange
1 fruit Exchange
1/2 fat Exchange

LEMON POPPYSEED SCONES

A tangy little treat that is really yummy with lemon curd.
(or my lemon filling/lemon curd)

> 1 2/3 cup flour
> 1 1/2 tsp. baking powder
> 1/2 tsp. baking soda
> 1/3 cup fruit sweetener
> 1/4 cup lemon juice
> 2 Tbsp. oil
> 1/3 cup nonfat plain yogurt
> 1 egg white
> small amount milk, if needed
> 2 tsp. poppy seeds
> 2 tsp. lemon zest

In large bowl, blend together first three ingredients.
In separate bowl, combine fruit sweetener, lemon juice,
oil, and yogurt. Beat in egg white. Pour this mixture into
dry ingredients and stir until smooth. Add poppy seeds and
lemon zest. Turn out on to floured surface and knead dough
a few times until it is smooth. Form dough into 10" circle
and transfer to baking sheet which has been sprayed with
non-stick coating. Mark dough lightly into 10 wedges. Bake
at 375 degrees for 12-15 minutes. Drizzle scones with
mixture of 1 Tbsp. lemon juice and 1 Tbsp. fruit sweetener.

Cut into 10 wedges. 1 serving = 1 wedge

132 calories	3 grams fat
23 grams carb.	0 mg cholesterol
3 grams protein	102 mg sodium

1 starch/bread Exchange
1/2 fruit Exchange
1/2 fat Exchange

CARROT SPICE MUFFINS

2 Tbsp. oil
1/2 cup non-fat plain yogurt
1/2 cup fruit sweetener
1/4 cup pineapple or orange juice
1 egg white
1 tsp. vanilla
2 cups flour
2 tsp. baking soda
2 tsp. cinnamon
1/2 tsp. ginger
1/4 tsp. cloves
1 cup raw shredded carrots
1/3 cup chopped nuts

In a large bowl, combine first four ingredients and beat together until well combined. Add egg white and vanilla. In a separate medium bowl, mix together dry ingredients. After blending, add carrots and nuts. Stir flour mixture into wet ingredients, one third at a time, stirring well after each addition. Spoon batter into muffin tins which have been spray with non-stick spray. Bake at 350 degrees for 10-15 minutes.

Makes 15 muffins.

1 serving = 1 muffin

130 calories
20 grams carb.
3 grams protein

4 grams fat
tr mg cholesterol
122 mg sodium

1 starch/bread Exchange
1 fat Exchange

62

CHOCOLATE MUFFINS

I could not resist this one! Even though I am not as much
a chocoholic as I once was, I do like these little muffins.

> 4 Tbsp. cocoa
> 1/4 cup oil
> 2/3 cup non-fat plain yogurt
> 2/3 cup fruit sweetener
> 2 egg white, beaten
> 2 Tbsp. orange juice concentrate (or 1 oz.)
> 2 tsp. grated orange rind
> 1 tsp. vanilla
> 2 cups flour
> 1 tsp. baking soda
> 1/4 tsp. salt

In large bowl, combine cocoa and oil, stirring until well
blended. Add yogurt and sweetener, mixing well. Blend in egg
whites. Stir in orange concentrate, rind, and vanilla. When
well combined, add dry ingredients. Spoon batter into 12
muffin cups which have been sprayed with non-stick spray.
Bake at 350 degrees for 15 minutes or until muffins are set.
Do not over-cook.

1 serving = 1 muffin

170 calories	5 grams fat
28 grams carb.	1 mg cholesterol
4 grams protein	132 mg sodium

1 starch/bread Exchange
1 fruit Exchange
1 fat Exchange

CHOCOLATE RASPBERRY MUFFINS

Follow above directions. After spooning batter into
muffin tins, press teaspoonful of fruit sweetened
raspberry preserves into center of muffin. Bake as
directed.

OAT BRAN ORANGE MUFFINS

2 Tbsp. oil
2/3 cup fruit sweetener
1/3 cup orange juice concentrate
1/3 cup water
2/3 cup plain non-fat yogurt
2 cups flour
1/2 cup oat bran
1 1/2 tsp. baking soda
1/4 tsp. salt
2 tsp. fresh grated orange rind
1/2 cup golden raisins

In large bowl, stir together first five ingredients until well combined. In separate bowl, combine dry ingredients, except raisins. Add dry mixture 1/3 at a time to batter and beat after each addition. When batter is well blended, stir in raisins. Spoon mixture into 15 muffin cups which have been sprayed with non-stick coating. Top each muffin with 1/2 tsp. fruit sweetener and light sprinkle of grated orange rind. Bake at 350 degrees for 15-20 minutes.

Yield: 15 muffins. 1 serving = 1 muffin

144 calories
29 grams carb.
3 grams protein

3 grams fat
0 mg cholesterol
126 mg sodium

1 starch/bread Exchange
1 fruit Exchange
1/2 fat Exchange

CORN MUFFINS

These are terrific with chili. They freeze well, too.

- 1 1/4 cup flour
- 1 1/4 cup corn meal
- 1 tsp. baking powder
- 1/4 tsp. salt
- 2 Tbsp. fruit sweetener or apple juice concentrate
- 3 Tbsp. oil
- 3 egg whites
- 1 1/4 cup skim milk

In large bowl, combine dry ingredients, mixing until well combined. In separate bowl, beat together remaining ingredients. When well blended, add this to dry mixture. Spoon batter into 10 muffin tins which have been sprayed with non-stick coating. Bake at 350 degrees for 15 minutes.

10 muffins. 1 serving = 1 muffin.

To make Mexi-cheese muffins, add 1/4 cup shredded cheddar cheese and 1/4 cup drained chopped green chilies to batter.

172 calories	5 grams fat
27 grams carb.	0 mg cholesterol
5 grams protein	124 mg sodium

1 starch/bread Exchange
1 fruit Exchange
1 fat Exchange

CRANBERRY ORANGE MUFFINS

If you are able to find dried fruit juice sweetened or just dried cranberries with no sweetener, both will work great. You may use regular cranberries. I usually chop them in the blender or food processor when they are still frozen. It works great!

2/3 cup fruit sweetener
1/2 cup orange juice
2 Tbsp. oil
2/3 cup non-fat plain yogurt
3 egg whites
2 tsp. fresh orange rind
2 cups flour
1 tsp. baking powder
1/4 tsp. baking soda
1/8 tsp. salt
1 cup chopped cranberries, regular or 2/3 cup dried

In large bowl, beat together first six ingredients. In separate bowl, combine remaining ingredients, except cranberries. When well blended, stir dry ingredients into wet mixture. Fold in cranberries. Spoon mixture into 12 muffins cups which have been sprayed with non-stick coating. Bake 12-15 minutes at 350 degrees.

1 serving = 1 muffin.

152 calories	3 grams fat
28 grams carb.	0 mg cholesterol
4 grams protein	89 mg sodium

1 starch/bread Exchange
1/2 fruit Exchange
1/2 fat Exchange

MIAMI MUFFINS

This is a moist low-fat muffin. I like it almost as much as Miami. I like to do this muffin with several kinds of fruit.

- 1/2 cup fruit sweetener
- 2 Tbsp. Canola oil
- 1/2 cup non-fat plain yogurt
- 1 egg white
- 1/4 cup orange juice
- 2 cups flour
- 1 1/2 tsp. baking powder
- 1/2 tsp. baking soda
- 1/8 tsp. salt
- 1/2 tsp. nutmeg
- 1/2 cup chopped fresh mango
- 1/4 cup chopped dried apricots
- 1/4 cup chopped toasted almonds (optional)

In a large bowl, combine the first three ingredients and stir until smooth. Blend in egg white and juice until mixture is smooth. In medium bowl, combine dry ingredients, blending well. Stir in fruit (and nuts, if desired). Spoon batter into muffin tins which have been sprayed with non-stick spray. Bake at 350 degrees for 10-15 minutes.

Makes 12 large muffins. 1 serving = 1 muffin

142 calories
26 grams carb.
3 grams protein

3 grams fat
1 mg cholesterol
105 mg sodium

1 starch/bread Exchange
1/2 fruit Exchange
1 fat exchange

MORNING GLORY MUFFINS

These remind me of a sunny morning ... yummy too.

2 Tbsp. oil
1/4 cup fruit sweetener
2/3 cup non-fat plain yogurt
1 egg white
2 cups flour
1 1/2 tsp. baking powder
1/2 tsp. baking soda
1/8 tsp. salt
1 small can unsweetened crushed pineapple and juice
1 orange, finely chopped
1/2 mango (or peach), finely chopped

In large bowl, combine first four ingredients. Mix together until well blended. In separate bowl, mix dry ingredients together, then add to wet mixture. Finally, add fruit, blending well. Spoon batter into muffin tins which have been sprayed with non-stick coating. Bake 15 minutes at 350 degrees.

Makes 12 muffins. 1 serving = 1 muffin

141 calories	3 grams fat
326 grams carb.	tr mg cholesterol
3 grams protein	134 mg sodium

1 starch/bread Exchange
1/2 fruit Exchange
1/2 fat Exchange

PEACH MUFFINS

A different idea for a muffin, but very moist and tasty.
If you find fruit sweetened desserts and breads too heavy
or moist for your taste, you might substitute part
granulated fructose for sweetener.

          2 Tbsp. oil
          1/2 cup fruit sweetener
          2 egg whites
          1/3 cup non-fat plain yogurt
          2 cups flour
          1/2 cup oat bran
          1 tsp. baking soda
          1/4 tsp. salt
          1 cup fresh peaches, finely chopped
          1/4 cup pecans, chopped, toasted (optional)

In a large bowl, beat together oil, fruit sweetener, egg
whites, and yogurt. Set aside. In medium bowl, combine next
four ingredients. When well blended, stir dry ingredients
into batter, 1/3 at a time. Finally, fold in peaches and
pecans. Spray muffin tin with non-stick spray. Fill muffin
tin cups 2/3 full with batter. Bake 15-20 minutes at 350
degrees.

Makes 16 muffins. 1 serving = 1 muffin

108 calories   2 grams fat
20 grams carb.   0 mg cholesterol
3 grams protein   95 mg sodium

1 fruit Exchange
1/2 starch/bread Exchange

PUMPKIN MUFFINS

This is one of the most popular Autumn muffins at the Coffee Connection in Issaquah. Thank you Kim and Teresa!! It can be made without the cream cheese, but that is my favorite part.

>   1/4 cup oil
>   2/3 cup fruit sweetener
>   2 cups pumpkin (1 - 16 oz. can)
>   1/2 cup skim milk
>   3 egg whites, slightly beaten
>   2 3/4 cup flour
>   1 tsp. baking powder
>   1/4 tsp. salt
>   1 tsp. cinnamon
>   1/2 tsp. ginger
>   1/2 tsp. cloves

Filling: (optional)
>   3 oz. light cream cheese (5 grams fat per oz.)
>   3 Tbsp. fruit sweetener
>   1 tsp. vanilla

In a large bowl, combine oil, fruit sweetener, and pumpkin. Stir until well blended. Slowly, add milk and egg whites, continuing to stir. In separate bowl, combine all dry ingredients and blend well. Stir dry ingredients into wet ingredients. When well combined, spoon batter into 18 muff cups which have been sprayed with non-stick spray. Filling: In small bowl, cream together cheese, fruit sweetener, and vanilla. With spoon, press a dollop of cheese filling into center of each muffin. Bake 15 minutes at 350 degrees.

1 serving = 1 muffin

125 calories	4 grams fat
20 grams carb.	2 mg cholesterol
3 grams protein	87 mg sodium

1 starch/bread Exchange
1 fat Exchange

CHALLAH

This is a new twist on a recipe that has been one of my favorites for years. The orange flavor adds a spark!

1 cup warm water
3 packets dry yeast
1 cup orange juice
1 Tbsp. butter, melted
1 Tbsp. oil
2/3 cup fruit sweetener
1/2 tsp. salt
2 tsp. fresh grated orange rind
1 egg
2 egg whites
7 cups unbleached flour
2 Tbsp. fresh orange rind
    or sesame seeds for topping

In small bowl, combine warm water and yeast. Blend together and set aside. In large bowl, combine next six ingredients, mixing until well combined. Add yeast mixture and blend well. Beat in egg and egg whites. Add flour 1/3 at a time, mixing well after each addition. Place dough on floured board and knead for about 3-5 minutes, adding flour if necessary to keep dough from being sticky. Continue kneading until dough is no longer sticky. Wash and dry mixing bowl and coat with 1/2 tsp. oil. Place dough into bowl, cover with towel, and let rise one hour. Punch down and let rise one additional hour. Preheat oven to 350 degrees. Divide dough in half. Divide each portion into thirds. Roll into three strips and braid together. Place on heavy baking sheet. Repeat with second half of dough. Sprinkle top of each loaf with orange rind or sesame seeds. Bake 25-30 minutes or until golden brown. Makes 2 challah. Each loaf yields 16 slices.

Total yield: 32 pieces. 1 serving = 1 slice.

128 calories	1 grams fat
25 grams carb.	7 mg cholesterol
4 grams protein	43 mg sodium

1 3/4 Bread/Starch Exchange

DILL BREAD

This is a great treat on a cold autumn evening with
creamy French vegetable soup.

> 1 package dry yeast
> 1/3 cup warm water
> 1 cup low-fat cottage cheese, at room temperature
> 3 Tbsp. oil
> 2 Tbsp. fruit sweetener
>   or frozen apple juice concentrate
> 1 egg or 2 egg whites
> 1 Tbsp. dry minced onion
> 2 tsp. dill seed
> 1/2 tsp. salt
> 1/4 tsp. baking soda
> 2 1/2 cups unbleached flour

Combine yeast and warm water, set aside. In large bowl,
combine cottage cheese, oil, and fruit juice sweetener,
stirring until well blended. Add yeast/water mixture. Beat
in egg whites. In separate bowl, combine dry ingredients.
Stir dry mixture into wet mixture. On floured pastry cloth,
knead dough 5 minutes. Set dough in clean bowl which has
been coated with 1/2 tsp. oil. Let rise 1 hour. Shape into
loaf, place in lightly oiled loaf pan, and let rise 30-40
minutes. Brush lightly with beaten egg white, sprinkle with
dill, and bake 40 minutes at 350 degrees.

1 loaf yields 14 slices. 1 serving = 1 slice.

124 calories	4 grams fat
18 grams carb.	16 mg cholesterol
5 grams protein	161 mg sodium

1 starch/bread Exchange
1 fat Exchange

CHEESE BREAD BRAID

I don't know where this recipe came from, but I have
had it forever. It can be made in single jelly roll
loaves for snacks.

    4 cups flour
    2 pkg. dry yeast
    1/4 cup fruit sweetener or fruit juice concentrate
    1 tsp. salt
    3/4 cup water
    1/2 cup milk
    2 Tbsp. oil
    1 egg

Filling:
    3 Tbsp. margarine, melted
    1 cup onion, finely chopped
    1 Tbsp. Parmesan cheese
    2 cloves garlic, minced
    1 tsp. paprika

In large bowl, combine flour and yeast. In saucepan,
combine fruit sweetener, salt, water, milk, and oil.
Heat until mixture is just warm. Pour liquid over flour
mixture and blend well. Add egg and beat 2 minutes. Cover
dough and let rise until double, about 45 minutes. In small
bowl, prepare filling. Roll out dough into 12" x 18"
rectangle and spread with filling. Roll up jelly roll
fashion. Place on lightly oiled cookie sheet. Cover and
let rise until double. Bake 35 minutes at 350 degrees.
For mini loaves, cut 12" x 18" rectangle into thirds.
Roll each third into mini loaf. Reduce baking time to
15-20 minutes.

Regular size loaf make 20 slices. 1 serving = 1 slice.

140 calories   4 grams fat
23 grams carb.   10 mg cholesterol
4 grams protein   140 mg sodium

1 1/2 Bread/Starch Exchange
1 Fat Exchange

GARLIC FRENCH BREAD

This is delicious, but bring your breath mints with you! Wow! If you like garlic you'll love this. I often roast my own garlic ahead of time or you may use raw crushed garlic or garlic in a jar.

> 2 Tbsp. margarine, melted
> 1/2 cup non-fat mayonnaise
> 1/4 cup fresh grated Parmesan
> 2-3 cloves garlic, crushed
> parsley
> paprika

Cut one (16 oz.) loaf of sourdough bread in half, lengthwise. Set aside. Combine the first four ingredients in a small bowl and blend well. With spatula, spread half of mixture on half of the loaf. Spread remaining mixture on the other half. Sprinkle each section with parsley and paprika. Broil until bubbly. Slice and serve.

16 servings. 1 serving = 1 slice

100 calories	3 grams fat
14 grams carb.	1 mg cholesterol
3 grams protein	0 mg sodium

1 starch/bread Exchange
1/2 fat Exchange

BLUEBERRY ORANGE BREAD

The Northwest has an abundance of wonderful berries.
August is the month for blackberries and blueberries.
This is a great treat using fresh or frozen berries.

    3 cups flour
    2 tsp. baking powder
    1/2 tsp. baking soda
    1 cup orange juice
    2/3 cup fruit sweetener
    1/4 cup oil
    2 egg whites
    2 tsp. grated orange rind
    1 cup blueberries

In large bowl, combine first three ingredients. In separate
bowl, blend together orange juice, fruit sweetener, and oil.
When well combined, add to flour mixture. Beat in egg whites
and orange rind. Fold in blueberries. Pour batter into loaf
pan which has been sprayed with non-stick spray. Bake at 350
degrees for 45-55 minutes.

Makes 16 slices. 1 serving = 1 slice

156 calories   4 grams fat
28 grams carb.   0 mg cholesterol
3 grams protein   75 mg sodium

1 starch/bread Exchange
1 fruit Exchange
1 fat Exchange

PEACH JAM

This formula will work with plums, too.

>4 1/4 cups peach pulp and sweetener combined*
>2 Tbsp. lemon juice
>1 pkg. pectin for low sugar jam

* I usually use about 3 1/2 cups fruit pulp and 3/4 cup fruit sweetener. The recipe is analyzed that way. Do it to your own tastes. Because the sweetener is a liquid and does not crystallize, it needs to be included in the 4 1/4 cups. (I have not tried jams using part granulated fructose, but that might be fun to try.)

Peel, pit, and crush fruit into pulp. Measure peaches, sweetener, and lemon juice into 4 quart saucepan. Slowly, add pectin, stirring until it is well dissolved. Place mixture over medium heat. Stirring constantly. Bring to boil; boil 1 minute. Remove from heat. Cool. Skim foam off top. Pour into container and seal. I use glass containers and freeze the jam. You may seal with paraffin.

Yield: 3 3/4 cups. 1 serving = 2 tsp.

10 calories	0 grams fat
0 grams carb.	0 mg cholesterol
0 grams protein	0 mg sodium

1 free food Exchange

ORANGE MARMALADE

This reminds me of the wonderful English marmalade that has a bit of a bite to it. Even those who don't love marmalade, love this. It is my favorite on crumpets. A great tradition in Victoria B.C.

> 3 large oranges with peel
> 1 1/2 cups water
> 1 1/4 cup fruit sweetener
> 1/3 cup orange juice concentrate
> 1 pkg. pectin (for use with low or no sugar)

Cut 1/4" from each end of orange and discard. Cut orange in 4-6 sections. Remove peel. Save peel, but discard as much of the thick white part as possible. (It is bitter.) Slice peel into small, thin pieces. In food processor, combine all ingredients, except peel and pectin. When well chopped, pour into 3 quart sauce pan. Stir in pectin until dissolved. Add peel. Bring mixture to boil and boil 2 minutes. Lower heat and simmer mixture for approximately one hour. If too much liquid evaporates, add just a bit bore water. When mixture is very thick and orange peel is tender, remove from heat. Cool. Pour into glass or plastic containers and freeze.

Makes approximately 2 1/2 cups. 1 serving = 2 tsp.

21 calories	tr grams fat
5 grams carb.	0 mg cholesterol
tr grams protein	tr mg sodium

1/3 fruit Exchange

STRAWBERRY JAM

I have received many requests for jams. This one is easy and delicious. I like it best as a frozen jam. It tastes really fresh! It should work well with other berries, too.

        4 cups mashed strawberries and fruit
            sweetener combined.
        (I use 3 cups berries plus 1 cup sweetener.)
        1 pkg. pectin for low sugar jams.

Combine fruit and sweetener in 4 quart sauce pan. Stir well to blend. Slowly, add pectin, stirring until it is completely dissolved. Place mixture over medium heat and bring to boil. Stir constantly to prevent burning. Boil hard for one minute. Remove from heat and cool. Skim top. Pour into glass jars. Cool. Top with paraffin. If freezing jam, you may just put on lid.

Yield: 4 cups. 1 serving = 2 tsp.

If using blueberries, add 2 Tbsp. lemon juice.

10 calories	0 grams fat
3 grams carb.	0 mg cholesterol
0 grams protein	0 mg sodium

1 free food Exchange

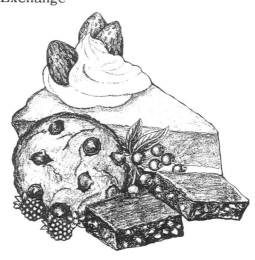

ENTREES

FETTUCINE PRIMAVERA

The foods that I love most always seem to include some super fattening sauce. I think fat is more difficult to avoid than sugar. I have attempted to drastically lower the fat in this recipe without sacrificing taste.

This is a quicky, so have the pasta water started as you prepare the sauce. Chop veggies ahead of time.

> 1 (9 oz.) pkg. fettucine pasta
> 4 tsp. oil
> 2-3 cloves garlic, crushed
> 3 Tbsp. dry minced onion
> 3 Tbsp. cornstarch
> 1 1/2 cups chicken broth, unsalted
> 1/2 cup 2% milk
> white pepper to taste
> 1/8 tsp. nutmeg
> 1/3 cup shredded cheese (bel paese, fontina,
>   gorgonzola combination is good)
> 2 cups chopped veggies: broccoli, carrots,
>   cherry tomatoes, onions
> 10 black olives, sliced
> 2 oz. Parmesan cheese, shredded

In large saucepan, over medium high heat, saute garlic and minced onion lightly. Remove from heat, stir in cornstarch and small amount of broth. Blend until smooth. Add remaining broth and continue stirring. Return pan to medium high heat and add milk, spices, and 1/3 cup of mixed cheeses. When cheese is melted and sauce well heated, remove from stove and cover. Cook pasta according to package. Vegetables may be steamed lightly in separate pan or added to sauce the last 2 minutes of simmering. Spoon pasta onto plates and top with sauce. Garnish with sliced black olives and Parmesan cheese.

6 servings. Makes approx. 6 cups. 1 serving = approx. 1 cup

298 calories	9 grams fat
43 grams carb.	15 mg cholesterol
13 grams protein	274 mg sodium

2 starch/bread Exchanges
1 vegetable Exchange; 2 fat Exchanges

INDY LASAGNA

This lasagna may be made without the Canadian bacon, however, it does add a nice flavor. This was inspired by a limousine driver in Indianapolis who believes that low-fat is a way of life.

> 1 recipe Marinara sauce (from this book)
>   or one 26 oz. jar
> 1 onion, chopped
> 3 cloves garlic, crushed
> 1/3 cup Canadian bacon or low-fat ham, chopped fine
> 2 pkg. frozen chopped spinach, thawed (or 1 large
>   bunch fresh spinach)
> 1/2 lb. mushrooms, sliced
> 2 cups low-fat ricotta cheese
> 1 cup low-fat mozzarella, shredded
> 12 lasagna noodles (12 oz.)
> 1/4 cup Parmesan cheese

If using homemade marinara sauce, prepare ahead of time. In large skillet, saute onion and garlic in 1 tsp. oil until golden. Add Canadian bacon and saute 2 minutes. Stir in spinach and mushrooms; simmer until well blended. Remove from heat and set aside. Prepare cheeses. Boil noodles according to directions on pkg. Spray 9" x 13" baking dish with non-stick spray. Layer ingredients, beginning with thin layer of sauce, then noodles, sauce, spinach, cheeses, noodles etc. using all ingredients (3 or 4 layers) ending with cheese. Sprinkle top with Parmesan. Bake 45-60 minutes at 350 degrees.

Makes 12 pieces. 1 serving = 1 piece

248 calories	6 grams fat
33 grams carb.	46 mg cholesterol
16 grams protein	328 mg sodium

2 starch/bread Exchanges
1 medium fat meat Exchange

JAN AND CAP'S PASTA

This is a simple great idea for pasta that was shared by talented artist Jan Hurd of Atherton, California. The subjects of her beautiful artwork are the flowers, fruits, and vegetables she grows! She and her husband, Cap, apply their art talents in the kitchen in a very healthy way!

> 1 - 9 oz. pkg. angel hair pasta (or your favorite)
> 4 cups raw vegetables, chopped
> 3 Tbsp. olive oil (I often use only 2)
> Fresh spices of your choice: basil, oregano, & garlic
> Top with small amount of fresh Parmesan

Cook pasta per package directions. When pasta is done, quickly, add chopped vegetables to pasta and water. Continue boiling for 30 seconds to 1 minute, just to blanch vegetables. Drain entire mixture in colander, then transfer to large bowl. Toss in oil, spices, and garlic. Sprinkle each serving with Parmesan.

Yield: 4 servings. 1 serving = approx. 1 1/4 cup

360 calories	11 grams fat
55 grams carb.	0 mg cholesterol
10 grams protein	25 mg sodium

3 starch/bread Exchanges
2 vegetable Exchanges
2 fat Exchanges

MOSSTACIOLI WITH HAZELNUTS & GORGONZOLA

This is a dish that I just love. It is so rich
in its original form that I can eat only a small
portion. The hazelnuts & gorgonzola do contain lots
of fat, so I have used very little. Since both have
lots of flavor, just a little is necessary.

> 1 recipe Healthy Cream Sauce
> 1 - 8 oz. pkg. mosstacioli pasta or fettucini
> 3 oz. gorgonzola cheese
> 8 Tbsp. hazelnuts, toasted, chopped

Make 1 recipe Healthy Cream Sauce. Cook pasta according
to package directions. Just before serving, crumble cheese
into cream sauce. Mix well. Divide noodles into 4 portions.
Top each portion with 1/2 cup sauce. Top each serving with
2 Tbsp. hazelnuts. Sprinkle with fresh chopped parsley.

4 Servings. 1 serving = 2 oz. dry pasta (6 oz. cooked)
plus 1/2 cup sauce.

420 calories	16 grams fat
51 grams carb.	15 mg cholesterol
16 grams protein	223 mg sodium

3 Bread/Starch Exchange
1 med. fat meat Exchange
2 Fat Exchange

PASTITSIO

I call this Greek Lasagna. I love the Mediterranean
flavors. This boasts the flavors without the fats.

Sauce: Prepare the Healthy Cream Sauce. Set aside.

Layer #1:
  1 - 16 oz. tubular pasta: ziti or mosstacioli
      cooked and cooled slightly
  3 egg whites, beaten until fluffy
  1 cup low-fat ricotta
  2/3 cup shredded Parmesan

Layer #2
  1 tsp. oil
  1 1/2 onion, chopped
  2 cloves garlic, chopped
  1/2 lb. extra lean ground beef
  1/2 lb. ground turkey breast
  1 - 14 oz. can low sodium tomato pieces
      with puree or tomatoes
  2 Tbsp. red wine
  1/2 tsp. basil
  1 tsp. oregano
  1/4 tsp. cinnamon
  1/4 tsp. salt, pepper to taste

Prepare sauce and refrigerate covered while preparing layers
1 & 2. Combine pasta with egg whites and cheeses. Refrigerate
while preparing layer 2. In large skillet, saute onion and
garlic until golden. Add meat and brown, stirring with fork
to blend meats. Add tomatoes, wine, and spices. In 9" x 13"
glass baking dish, spread thin layer of sauce in bottom.
Next layer pasta, meat mixture, then remaining sauce. Bake
1 hour at 350 degrees.

Yield:12 servings. 1 serving = 1 1/4 cup.

275 calories	7 grams fat
32 grams carb.	34 mg cholesterol
19 grams protein	222 mg sodium

2 starch/bread Exchanges
2 low-fat meat Exchanges

CALICO CHILI WITH WHEAT BERRIES

This chili gets its name from the variety of beans used in it. It is a vegetarian chili filled with flavor and lots of goodies. You may substitute barley for wheat berries.

    1 tsp. oil
    1 large onion, chopped
    2-3 cloves garlic, minced
    2-15 oz. cans tomatoes
    1/2 cup water
    1 tsp. chili powder
    1 tsp. cumin
    1/2 tsp. oregano
    1/4 tsp. salt
    1 cup wheat berries, pre-cooked (see grains & rice)
    1 - 15 oz. can each: garbanzo beans, kidney beans,
        pinto beans, and navy beans
    1 cup celery, chopped
    1 red pepper, chopped
    1 green pepper, chopped
    1 small can sliced black olives

In large kettle, saute onion and garlic until golden. Add tomatoes, spices, and wheat berries. Simmer over medium heat for 30 minutes. Add beans and vegetables, except olives. Simmer additional 20 minutes to blend flavors. Add olives, heat and serve. If chili becomes too thick, thin slightly with water.

Yield: 16 cups. 1 serving = 1 cup.
Serve with corn bread or corn muffins.

140 calories	2 grams fat
26 grams carb.	0 mg cholesterol
7 grams protein	620 mg sodium

1 1/2 Bread/Starch Exchanges

CHILI ON THE WILD SIDE

This chili is very spicy. You may wish to tone down the spices if it is too wild!

1 tsp. oil
1 onion, finely chopped
2 cloves garlic, minced
1/2 lb. extra lean ground beef
1/2 lb. ground turkey breast
1 - 15 oz. can tomato sauce, no salt
1 - 14 1/2 oz. can tomatoes
1 cup water
1 - 4 oz. can diced green chilies
1 tsp. Worchestershire sauce
1 tsp. chili powder
1 tsp. cumin
1/2 tsp. cinnamon
1/2 tsp. oregano
1/4 tsp. ground cloves
1/4 tsp. salt.
2 - 15 oz. cans pinto beans, rinsed & drained well
2 - 15 oz. cans kidney beans, rinsed & drained well

In large kettle or Dutch oven, saute onion & garlic in oil. When translucent, add ground meats and brown well. Add remaining ingredients, except beans, and simmer over medium heat 1 hour. If chili cooks down too much add more water. Add beans and simmer an additional 20 minutes.

Yield: 16 cups. 1 serving = 1 cup

155 calories   3 grams fat
21 grams carb.   15 mg cholesterol
11 grams protein   440 mg sodium

1 1/2 starch/bread Exchanges
1 low-fat meat Exchange

85

CRAB CAKES

This is a very simple version of crab cakes. It can also be made using shrimp. Since fresh seafood is hard to come by in many parts of the country, I have done the recipe with canned crab.

        1 - 6 oz. can crab meat, rinsed and drained
        2 tsp. lemon juice
        1 cup celery, finely chopped
        5-6 scallions, chopped
        1 egg white, lightly beaten
        3/4 cup bread crumbs, with Italian seasoning
        1/4 tsp. garlic powder
        1/4 tsp. salt, pepper to taste
        2 tsp. oil

Another option is salmon. If you make salmon patties, add 1/2 tsp. dill weed.

In large bowl, combine crab, lemon juice, celery, and and scallions. When well mixed, stir in egg white, bread crumbs, and spices. You may want to use your hands for this. Shape into four large patties. Place oil in large skillet over medium high heat. Brown patties on both sides. Reduce heat. Simmer for 10 minutes over medium heat or until patties are thoroughly heated. Serve with Seafood Sauce (see recipe), rice, salad, and hot sour dough bread.

4 servings. 1 serving = 1 patty.

156 calories	4 grams fat
18 grams carb.	43 mg cholesterol
12 grams protein	525 mg sodium

1 starch/bread Exchange
1 medium fat meat Exchange

SEAFOOD SAUTE

This is very colorful, tasty, and light. It is, also, rich and flavorful. A good dish to serve special guests.

> 3-4 Roma or regular tomatoes, diced*
> 1 tsp. oil
> 5 scallions, chopped
> 2 cloves garlic, minced
> 2/3 cup celery, chopped
> 1 tsp. lemon pepper herb combo (Mrs. Dash type)
> 1 cup shrimp, crab, or salmon (canned, rinsed)
> 10 stuffed green olives, sliced
> 2 tsp. fresh parsley
> 1/4 tsp. dill weed (optional)

* If desired use 1 - 14.5 oz. can low sodium tomatoes.

Prepare tomatoes, set aside. In large skillet, over medium heat saute scallions, garlic, and celery for 3 minutes. (Keep it crisp) Add pepper, crab, olives, parsley, and dill. When well combined, add tomatoes and cook until all ingredients are hot. Serve over pasta, rice, new potatoes.

2 servings. 1 serving = approx. 1 cup
147 calories   4 grams fat
12 grams carb.   111 mg cholesterol
19 grams protein   160 mg sodium

2 low-fat meat Exchanges
2 vegetable Exchanges

PITA BREAD WITH CRAB FILLING

This is a simple, tasty, dish which can be made with fresh or canned seafood.

> 1 cup celery, chopped
> 10 green or black olives, sliced
> 6 scallions, chopped
> 2 Tbsp. bread crumbs
> 1/4 cup non-fat yogurt
> 1/4 cup non-fat mayonnaise
> pepper to taste
> 1 - 6 oz. can crab meat (rinse well)
>   or 1 - 4 oz. can shrimp
> 2 pieces pita bread, cut in half
> 4 tsp. Parmesan cheese, grated

Combine first seven ingredients in large skillet, stirring over medium heat until mixture is bubbly. Reduce heat, add crab and continue simmering 3-5 minutes. Spoon into heated pita bread halves. Sprinkle each with 1 tsp. Parmesan.

Makes 4 sandwiches. 1 serving = 1 sandwich

154 calories   4 grams fat
18 grams carb.   45 mg cholesterol
12 grams protein   515 mg sodium

1 starch/bread Exchange
2 low-fat meat Exchanges

ARTICHOKE CHICKEN CASSEROLE

A tasty dish inspired by Carole McGavick. I tried
to take out calories yet preserve the taste.

> 2 - 10 oz. pkg. chopped spinach
> 2 cups cooked rice
> 2 egg whites
> 4 single chicken breasts (12 oz. cooked weight)
>   cooked and cubed
> 1 - 15 oz. jar artichoke hearts (in water)
>   drained and chopped
> 1 recipe healthy cream sauce
> 2 cloves garlic, crushed
> 1 1/2 tsp. poultry seasoning
> 2 Tbsp. dehydrated chopped onion
> 1 cup sliced fresh mushrooms
> 1 cup shredded low-fat cheddar cheese

Spray 9" x 13" glass baking dish with non-stick coating.
In large bowl, combine first three ingredients. Press into
bottom of baking dish as a crust. On top of spinach mixture,
layer chicken, then artichokes; refrigerate covered. In
large saucepan, make cream sauce. Stir in spices, onion,
and mushrooms. Pour over spinach chicken mixture. Top with
shredded cheese. Bake at 350 degrees 45-55 minutes or until
hot and bubbly in center.

12 servings. 1 serving= 1 1/4 cup.

172 calories	4 grams fat
20 grams carb.	35 mg cholesterol
16 grams protein	165 mg sodium

1 starch/bread Exchange
2 low-fat meat Exchanges

CHICKEN POT PIE

Made the old fashioned way, this dish is in a heavy cream sauce with a rich, fat filled crust. This recipe brightens the flavors and cuts the creams and fats.

>4 single chicken breasts, precooked, and cut into 1" chunks (12 oz. cooked weight)
>1 tsp. oil
>1 onion, chopped
>3 red potatoes(6 oz. ea.),cut in 1/2" chunks
>4 carrots, diced
>1 cup fresh or frozen peas
>3 Tbsp. fresh parsley
>3 Tbsp. pimento, finely minced
>2 tsp. capers
>1/2 - 1 tsp. salt free spice combination
>1 recipe healthy cream sauce

Crust:
>1 cup flour
>1/4 cup instant potato flakes
>2 Tbsp. grated Parmesan cheese
>2 Tbsp. oil
>1/4 tsp. salt

Prepare chicken, set aside. In large skillet, saute onion in oil until soft. Add potatoes, carrots and 2/3 cup water. Simmer vegetables in water until they are partially cooked (add more water if necessary). Add peas, spices, chicken, and cream sauce. Mix well and spoon into 2 or 3 quart souffle dish. In medium bowl, combine crust ingredients, adding 2-3 Tbsp. water to make dough workabl Roll out dough on floured surface. Roll into circle slightly larger than souffle dish. Place crust on top of chicken mixture. Trim and flute crust edges. Bake at 325 degrees for 45-55 minutes or until golden and bubbly.

Makes 8 servings. 1 serving= 1 cup

257 calories	7 grams fat
29 grams carb.	37 mg cholesterol
18 grams protein	187 mg sodium

2 starch/bread Exchanges
2 low-fat meat Exchanges

CHICKEN CACCIATORE

Usually Chicken Cacciatore uses the whole chicken. This version uses the chicken breast only. This is good with pasta, gnocchi, or rice.

> 4 single chicken breasts, boned, skinned, and washed, sliced in 1/2" strips (16 oz. raw weight)
> 3 tsp. oil
> 4 cloves garlic, minced
> 4 large onion, cut in strips
> 1 pound fresh mushrooms, cleaned, sliced
> 1 yellow pepper, cut in strips
> 1 green pepper, cut in strips
> 1 - 14.5 oz. can diced tomatoes in puree, low sodium
> 1/2 low sodium chicken broth
> 2 Tbsp. dry white wine
> 2 Tbsp. water
> 1/4 tsp. thyme
> 1/4 summer savory

In large skillet, heat oil to medium high. Brown chicken strips until golden on both sides. Reduce heat to medium low, add garlic and continue cooking until garlic is soft. Prepare vegetables and mix together in large bowl. Set aside. Stir tomatoes, broth, wine, water, and spices into chicken mixture. Simmer for 20 minutes over medium heat. Add prepared vegetables to skillet and stir in with wooden spoon. Cook until veggies are heated through, but still crisp and colorful. Serve with pasta of choice. Sprinkle lightly with fresh Parmesan. Use 2 tsp. Parmesan per serving.

4 large servings. 1 serving = 1 1/2 cup

273 calories   11 grams fat
23 grams carb.   55 mg cholesterol
25 grams protein   150 mg sodium

3 low-fat meat Exchanges
4 vegetable Exchanges

CAJUN CHICKEN

This is hot and spicy. It is quick to fix, attractive, and a nice company dish. When my brother, Jim, comes to Seattle on business, this is the dish that he loves. It also works well with shrimp.

> 4 single chicken breasts, (16 oz. raw weight) skinned, boned, washed, cut in 1" strips.
> 3 tsp. Canola oil
> 1/2 recipe Cajun spice sauce
> 1/2 cup water
> 1/4 cup Burgundy
> 1 large onion, cut in 1/4" strips
> 1 large red pepper, cut into 1/4" strips
> 1 lb. mushrooms, cleaned, peeled, sliced

In large deep skillet, saute chicken strips in oil. When well browned on both sides, add Cajun spice sauce, water, and Burgundy. Simmer over medium low heat for 20 minute until chicken is cooked through. Just 5 minutes before serving, add onion, pepper, and mushrooms. Simmer until veggies are just hot, but still crisp. Serve over rice.

Yield: 4 servings. 1 serving approx. 1 1/4 cup.

You may use yellow, red, and green peppers to add color. Veggies look and taste better if not over-cooked.

1 serving = 1/4 recipe

236 calories	9 grams fat
18 grams carb.	52 mg cholesterol
23 grams protein	64 mg sodium

3 low-fat meat Exchanges
3 vegetable Exchanges

CARIBBEAN CHICKEN

Another nice spicy company dish. This is easy to prepare at the last minute if you have the ingredients on hand.

        2 tsp. oil
        6 single chicken breasts (24 oz. raw weight)
                skinned, boned, washed, sliced in 1/2" strips
        2-3 cloves garlic, minced
        1/2 cup onion, chopped
        1/4 cup peach or apricot chutney (fruit sweetened)
        1/2 tsp. thyme
        1/2 tsp. each curry powder, cinnamon, nutmeg, cloves
        1/4 tsp. dry mustard
        1 1/2 cup low sodium chicken broth
        3 Tbsp. dry white wine
        2 tsp. coconut flavoring

In large skillet, heat oil to medium high, and saute chicken pieces until brown. Remove chicken, set aside. Saute garlic and onion in skillet until soft, and golden. Stir in chutney and spices and cook 1 minute. Add broth and wine, and heat through, stirring constantly. Return chicken to sauce, reduce heat, and simmer 15 minutes. Stir in coconut flavoring. Serve over hot rice.

6 servings. 1 serving = 1 1/4 cup.

160 calories	6 grams fat
6 grams carb.	52 mg cholesterol
19 grams protein	44 mg sodium

3 low-fat meat Exchanges
1/3 fruit Exchange

CURRY CHICKEN

This is a spicy dish. Good with white rice and
a colorful fresh fruit salad.

> 6 single chicken breasts, skinned, boned, washed
> (24 oz. raw weight)
> 3 tsp. oil
> 1/2 onion, chopped
> 2 cloves garlic, crushed
> 1/2 cup low sodium chicken broth
> 1 1/2 cup water
> 1/2 tsp. cumin
> 1/2 tsp. coriander
> 1/2 tsp. tumeric
> 1/8 tsp. allspice
> 1/8 tsp. ginger
> dash fennel
> dash black pepper
> 1 tsp. coconut flavoring

In large skillet, saute chicken breasts in 2 tsp. oil until
golden on both sides. Remove chicken from pan. Saute garl
and onion in remaining tsp. oil 5-7 minutes. Add broth,
water, and all of the spices to garlic-onion mixture. When
well blended, return chicken pieces to skillet. Cover and
simmer over medium heat for 30 minutes. Stir in coconut
flavoring. Serve over rice or rice/grain mixture.

6 Servings. 1 serving= 1 1/4 cup.

145 calories	6 grams fat
2 grams carb.	52 mg cholesterol
19 grams protein	43 mg sodium

3 low-fat meat Exchanges

DIJON CHICKEN PASTRIES

This recipe is somewhat like the regular chicken pastries in that it also uses the fillo dough. This recipe is one that my son came up with. It is really tasty. Thanks, Ron.

> 1 recipe Dijon sauce (see recipe)
> 1 pkg. frozen spinach, chopped and thawed
> 4 single chicken breasts, cooked and cubed
>   (12 oz. cooked)
> 2 cloves garlic, crushed
> 2 tsp. dry minced onion
> 1/4 tsp. salt
> pepper to taste
> 8 sheets fillo dough
> 3 tsp. margarine, melted

Make Dijon sauce and set aside. In large bowl, combine spinach, chicken, garlic, onion, salt and pepper. Set aside. Place 2 sheets of fillo dough on pastry cloth. With pastry brush, apply a thin coating of margarine over entire surface. Repeat this with two sheets of fillo at a time. Use margarine sparingly. Cut layered fillo into four squares. Place 1/4 of chicken mixture in strip near edge of each square. Spoon 2 Tbsp. Dijon sauce over each mound of chicken. Roll up each square and tuck ends under securely. Place on baking sheet Bake 15-20 minutes at 350 degrees. Serve with rice or gnocchi. Spoon 2 more Tbsp. Dijon sauce over each pastry and garnish with parsley.

4 servings. 1 serving = 1 pastry

350 calories   12 grams fat
28 grams carb.   72 mg cholesterol
31 grams protein   530 mg sodium

3 low-fat meat Exchanges
2 starch/bread Exchanges

FILLO CHICKEN WITH SPINACH

These little packages take less time to put together than you would imagine. A good dish for guests.

        6 single chicken breasts (24 oz. raw weight)
                boned, skinned, washed, sliced in 1/2" strips
        3 tsp. oil
        1 large onion, chopped
        2 cloves, garlic, minced
        1 - 10 oz. pkg. frozen chopped spinach, thawed
        1 1/2 cup sliced fresh mushrooms
        1 tsp. dill weed
        1 tsp. mint
        pepper to taste
        6 tsp. fresh Parmesan, grated
        12 pieces fillo dough
        6 tsp. margarine, melted

In large skillet, brown chicken pieces in 2 tsp. oil. Remove from pan and set aside. In remaining oil, saute onion and garlic, until golden. Add spinach, mushrooms, dill, mint, and pepper. Remove from heat and stir in chicken pieces. Cool mixture slightly. Place 2 pieces of fillo dough on working surface, such as pastry cloth. Brush top piece of fillo with 1 tsp. melted margarine. Divide chicken mixture into six portions. Place one portion in center of fillo dough. Fold sides of fillo over chicken mixture, then tuck ends under and place on heavy Teflon coated baking sheet. Repeat process with remaining fillo and chicken, making six packages. Brush tops of each fillo package with thin coat of margarine. Sprinkle top of each with 1 tsp. Parmesan. Bake at 325 degrees for 25 minutes or until golden brown.

Makes 6 servings. 1 serving = 1 pkg.

313 calories   14 grams fat
22 grams carb.   54 mg cholesterol
24 grams protein   328 mg sodium

1 starch/bread Exchange
3 low-fat meat Exchanges
1 fat Exchange

FLORENTINE CHICKEN BREASTS

This was inspired by a similar dish made by one of my artist's, Kay Barnes. She cooks low-fat gourmet for her whole family.

> 6 single chicken breasts (24 oz. raw weight)
>   skinned, boned, and washed
> 1 tsp. oil
> 1/4 cup finely chopped onion
> 2 cloves garlic, crushed
> 1 - 10 oz. pkg. frozen chopped spinach
> 1 1/2 cup sliced fresh mushrooms
> 1/2 tsp. basil
> 2 egg whites, beaten until frothy
> 3/4 cup bread crumbs
> 6 Tbsp. shredded Parmesan cheese or low-fat Swiss

Wash and pat dry the chicken breasts. Store covered in refrigerator while preparing filling. In large skillet, saute onion and garlic in oil. When onion is golden, add spinach, and mixed together well. Stir in mushrooms and basil. Remove from heat. Spoon half of egg white mixture into spinach, stirring until well combined. On large work surface, flatten chicken pieces. Dividing spinach mixture evenly, spoon portion onto each chicken breast. Roll chicken breasts and secure with toothpick, if necessary. Dip each breast in remaining egg white, then in bread crumbs. Place in 9" x 13" glass baking dish which has been sprayed with non-stick coating. Sprinkle each breast with 1 Tbsp. Parmesan cheese. Bake at 325 degrees for 30 minutes. Serve with rice, pasta, or new potatoes.

6 Servings. 1 serving = 1 stuffed chicken breast.

232 calories	8 grams fat
14 grams carb.	57 mg cholesterol
26 grams protein	312 mg sodium

3 low-fat meat Exchanges
1/2 starch/bread Exchange
1 vegetable Exchange

GARLIC CHICKEN

This chicken is great over rice or pasta. If I serve it over pasta, I garnish it with fresh parsley and sliced black olives.

    2 tsp. oil
    4 single chicken breasts (16 oz. raw weight)
        skinned, boned, washed, cut into 1" strips
    5-6 cloves garlic, sliced
    2 1/4 cups chicken broth, unsalted
    1/4 cup lemon juice
    1/3 cup dry white wine
    1/4 tsp. salt
    pepper to taste

In large skillet, heat oil to medium high. Stir fry chicken strips until well browned on both sides. Remove chicken pieces and set aside. Saute garlic slices until soft and golden. Stir in chicken broth, lemon juice, and wine. When mixture is hot, reduce heat to medium and return chicken to skillet. Simmer few minutes to heat through. If desired, thicken sauce with instant potatoes. Serve over rice.

Yield: 4 servings. 1 serving = 1/4 recipe

165 calories   7 grams fat
3 grams carb.   52 mg cholesterol
19 grams protein   178 mg sodium

3 low-fat meat Exchanges

CHICKEN PARMESAN

One of my favorite dishes. Anything Italian is one of
my favorites. I use tomato puree with tomato chunks. It
contains no sugar and less salt than most tomato sauce.

> 4 single chicken breasts (5 oz. each raw weight)
> skinned, boned, washed
> 2/3 cup Italian flavored bread crumbs
> 2 tsp. oil
> 2 cups tomato puree, no salt added
> 1 cup chicken broth, low sodium
> 1/2 tsp. each oregano, basil (fresh is always best)
> 2 cloves garlic, crushed
> 2 Tbsp. parsley, chopped
> 3 Tbsp. Burgundy
> 1/2 cup Parmesan cheese, grated, fresh

After washing chicken, set aside. Spread bread crumbs in
pie pan. Flatten each chicken breast and dip in small amount
of skim milk to dampen it. Place in pie pan, one piece at a
time and press crumbs into both sides of chicken until it
is well coated. Repeat with each piece. In large skillet,
heat oil to medium high. Add chicken breasts and brown
quickly on each side. When chicken is browned, reduce heat
to medium low. In large bowl, combine remaining ingredients
except Parmesan . Pour sauce over chicken and simmer 20-25
minutes. Serve over pasta, rice, or gnocchi. Sprinkle
small amount of Parmesan over each serving.

Yield: 4 servings. 1 serving = 1/4 recipe

350 calories	13 grams fat
26 grams carb.	75 mg cholesterol
33 grams protein	434 mg sodium

4 low-fat meat Exchanges
2 vegetable Exchanges
1 starch/ bread Exchange

CHICKEN PASTRIES

This is a recipe which I adapted from a delicious holiday dish by Karen Anderson and Marilyn Boucher. I loved the original, but the fat grams were the killer.

2 oz. fat free cream cheese
1 oz. low-fat cream cheese
2 Tbsp. skim milk
2 cups cooked, cubed chicken breast (8 oz.)
1 Tbsp. chopped chives
2 Tbsp. pimento, chopped
1/8 tsp. salt
1/4 tsp. pepper
8 sheets fillo (Phyllo) dough
3 tsp. margarine, melted

In large bowl, cream together cheeses and milk. When smooth, stir in chicken, chives, pimento, salt, and pepper. Set aside. On floured board, lay out 2 pieces of fillo. With pastry brush, spread thin coating of melted margarine over surface. Repeat this process, using 2 pieces of fillo at a time until you have all 8 pieces stacked. Use margarine sparingly so that every second layer will have a thin coating. Cut fillo stack into 4 large squares. Place 1/4 of chicken mixture in center of each square. Fold each square over into triangle and pinch edges tightly. Place on baking sheet. Bake 20 minutes at 350 degrees.

Yield: 4 pastries. 1 serving = 1 pastry

251 calories	8 grams fat
20 grams carb.	53 mg cholesterol
21 grams protein	428 mg sodium

1 starch/bread Exchange
3 low-fat meat Exchanges

TORTILLA CHICKEN FIESTA

The taste is rich, but the calories are cut by
using non-fat yogurt instead of sour cream,
and corn tortilla instead of chips. Inspired by
Juelle Edwards.

> 4 single chicken breasts, cooked and cut in 1"
>   chunks (12 oz. cooked weight)
> 1 1/2 cups non-fat yogurt
> 1/2 cup low-fat ricotta
> 2/3 cup low sodium chicken broth
> 1 - 4 oz. can diced green chilies
> 1 onion, chopped
> 1 can water chestnuts, sliced
> 1 dozen corn tortillas, cut into bite sized pieces
> 2/3 cup grated low-fat cheddar or Parmesan cheese

Prepare chicken and set aside. In large bowl, combine next
six ingredients in order, mixing well after each addition.
In 9" x 13" glass baking dish, which has been lightly sprayed
with non-stick spray, layer ingredients in the following
order: Thin layer of sauce, followed by tortilla pieces,
chicken pieces, remaining sauce, then top with even layer
of grated cheese. Bake 45-55 minutes at 325 degrees or until
bubbling in center. Cut into 12 squares.

1 serving = 1/12 of recipe.

178 calories	5 grams fat
19 grams carb.	34 mg cholesterol
16 grams protein	180 mg sodium

1 starch/bread Exchange
2 low-fat meat Exchanges

CHICKEN IN WINE SAUCE

This is an adaptation of a recipe given to me long ago. It originally had lots and lots of fat. Now the fat can stay on the butter cube instead of on my thighs. I like this version as well and I feel much healthier for not having eaten the extra 25 lbs. of butter over the last 10 years!

> 6 single chicken breasts (24 oz. raw weight) skinned, boned, and washed
> 1 tsp. butter
> 1 tsp. oil
> 3 Tbsp. cornstarch
> 1 1/2 chicken broth, unsalted
> 1/3 cup skim milk
> 1/3 cup lemon juice
> 1/3 cup dry white wine
> 3 cloves garlic, crushed
> 1/4 cup Parmesan cheese, fresh, grated

Prepare chicken breasts and set aside. Place butter in large skillet, heating to medium high. Brown chicken on both sides and remove from pan. Place chicken breasts in 9" x 13" glass baking dish which has been sprayed with non-stick spray. Pour oil into hot skillet. Stir in cornstarch and small amount of chicken broth. Stir until smooth. Remove pan from heat and, slowly, add 1 cup of broth. Return to heat, stir constantly, and add remaining broth, milk, lemon juice, wine, and garlic. When sauce has thicken slightly, pour over chicken breasts. Sprinkle Parmesan over chicken. Bake 30 minutes at 350 degrees. Serve over rice, pasta, or gnocchi.

Yield: 6 servings. 1 serving = 1 piece chicken with sauce

183 calories	7 grams fat
6 grams carb.	57 mg cholesterol
21 grams protein	135 mg sodium

3 low-fat meat Exchanges

TENDERLOIN IN CRANBERRY MARINADE

This is extremely easy to prepare. It is delicious as
a summer dish serve with white rice, green salad, fresh
fruit, and rolls. Other flavors of marinade will work.

> 1 cup fruit juice sweetened cranberry chutney
>   or marinade
> 2 Tbsp. rice vinegar
> 1/2 cup low sodium chicken broth
> 6 - 3 oz. lean pork tenderloin pieces

Reserve 1/2 cup of cranberry chutney to brush on finished
meat. Combine 1/2 cup cranberry chutney, vinegar, and
chicken broth in 9" square glass pan. Marinate pork pieces
1 hour on each side in this mixture (or overnight if desired).
Grill on barbecue 6-9 minutes per side or until done to your
liking. Brush finished meat with coating of chutney.

Makes 6 - 3 oz. servings.

180 calories	3 grams fat
18 grams carb.	60 mg cholesterol
19 grams protein	44 mg sodium

3 low-fat meat Exchanges
1 fruit Exchange

103

BEST BURGER

If you love having a burger, yet you are trying to cut
back on animal fats in your diet, it can be difficult
to find a tasty way to make one. When I get a craving
for a good tasting, good for you, burger, I make this.

> 1/2 lb. extra lean ground beef
> 1/2 lb. ground turkey breast
> 1 egg white
> 2/3 cup Italian flavored bread crumbs (choose the
>   brand that is lowest in sodium)
> 1 Tbsp. Worcestershire sauce
> 1 - 2 tsp. peppercorns or capers, if desired

In large bowl, combine beef and turkey, mixing together
with fork. Add egg white, bread crumbs, and Worcestershire
sauce, working this into meat until thoroughly combined.
Pat mixture into 4-5 burger patties. Grill on barbecue or
cook in skillet in 1 tsp. oil.

Makes 4 large patties. 1 serving = 1 patty

236 calories   8 grams fat
12 grams carb.   70 mg cholesterol
27 grams protein   223 mg sodium

1 starch/bread Exchange
3 low-fat meat Exchanges

FALAFEL BURGER

This is my favorite. Not being a big meat eater, I love
this Mediterranean flavored turkey burger. Very low in fat,
yet very flavorful. It is good eaten in a bun or fabulous
served on top of bulgar wheat or grain medley. (see recipe)

    3 oz. falafel mix (1/2 pkg.)
    2/3 cup water
    1/2 lb. ground turkey breast
    1 egg white

In large bowl, combine falafel mix and 2/3 cup water.
Add turkey and egg white, mixing well with fork. If
mixture is too dry, add more water to make it workable.
Form mixture into 4 patties. Fry in skillet in 1 tsp.
oil. Brown well on each side before turning.

This burger works better in a skillet than on a barbecue
grill. If you grill these do so on a small metal cookie
sheet or foil so that meat will not fall between the grill
wires.

Yield: 4 patties. 1 serving = 1 patty

157 calories   3 grams fat
13 grams carb.   35 mg cholesterol
19 grams protein   396 mg sodium

1 starch/bread Exchange
2 low-fat meat Exchanges

HEAVENLY CHEESEBURGER PIE

This giant size cheeseburger is fun for even kids to make.
It is fast, easy, and great for a party.

Filling:
  1/3 cup chopped onion
  1/2 lb. lean ground beef
  1/2 lb. ground turkey breast
  1/2 cup instant potato flakes
  1 egg white
  1/4 cup tomato sauce
  2 Tbsp. Dijon mustard
  1 dill pickle, finely chopped
  1/2 cup low-fat cheddar cheese
Crust:
  1/4 cup instant potato flakes
  2 cups flour
  1 Tbsp. fruit sweetener or granulated fructose
  1/2 tsp. baking soda
  2 Tbsp. melted margarine or butter
  1/4 cup fat free mayonnaise
  1/2 cup non-fat milk

Using large skillet, saute onion in 1 tsp. oil. When
transparent, add ground beef and turkey. Brown well.
Remove skillet from heat and add remaining ingredients,
except cheese. Set aside. In large bowl, combine first
four crust ingredients. Blend well with fork. Stir in
margarine, mayonnaise, and milk until well combined. Add
enough liquid so that dough holds together. Divide dough
in half and roll each half into 9-10" circle. Place one
circle on large pizza pan which has been sprayed with non-
stick coating. Spoon filling onto dough circle, spreading
evenly and leaving 1" of dough showing at edge. Sprinkle
cheese over meat mixture. Top with second circle of dough,
crimping top and bottom dough together around edges of pie
Optional: Sprinkle top of pie with mixture of 1/4 cup
potato flakes and 1 tsp. margarine. Bake at 350 degrees
30-40 minutes or until golden. Cut in 10 wedges.

Makes 10 servings. 1 serving = 1 wedge
236 calories   7 grams fat
25 grams carb.   37 mg cholesterol
7 grams protein   280 mg sodium
1 1/2 starch/bread Exchanges; 2 low-fat meat Exchanges

MEATBALLS

This is a good general recipe for a low-fat meatball which can be served by itself or in a variety of ways such as on pasta with sauce, in a marinade over rice, or in mushroom gravy with small red potatoes.

> 1/2 lb. extra lean ground beef
> 1/2 lab. ground turkey breast
> 2 egg whites
> 2 Tbsp. Parmesan cheese
> 1-2 cloves fresh garlic, crushed
> 1-2 tsp. chopped dry onion
> 2 tsp. parsley
> salt (optional)
> pepper to taste
> 1 1/4 cup bread crumbs
> 1/4 cup broth, unsalted (enough to moisten mixture)

In large bowl, combine ground meat and egg whites. Mix well with a fork or your fingers. (This is a "hands on" project) Add remaining ingredients, except liquid, and mix thoroughly. If using for an Italian dish, add 1 tsp. of basil, oregano, and fennel. Add enough broth to make mixture workable, but not too wet. Roll 1 1/2" balls and place on large platter. In large Teflon skillet, heat 1 tsp. oil to medium hot. Brown meat balls well on all sides. When meatballs are thoroughly cooked, cool and store for future use or use immediately.

Makes 25 meatballs. 1 serving = 5 meatballs

252 calories	8 grams fat
19 grams carb.	54 mg cholesterol
26 grams protein	294 mg sodium

1 starch/bread Exchange
3 meat Exchanges

MEAT LOAF AND MASHED POTATO PIE

My healthy version of something I disliked as a child. I could not imagine ever liking meat loaf, but the potatoes on top made it palatable for me. For Shari Wainberg: one of her comfort foods!

1/2 lb. extra lean ground beef
1/2 lb. ground turkey breast
1 egg white
1/4 cup broth, unsalted
2/3 cup bread crumbs
2 cloves garlic, crushed
3 Tbsp. onion, finely chopped
1 tsp. parsley
1 tsp. summer savory
1 tsp. capers (optional)
1/4 tsp. salt
pepper to taste
3 cups mashed potatoes (with 1/4 cup nonfat milk,
1/8 tsp. salt, and 1 Tbsp. margarine added)

In large bowl, combine meat, egg white, and broth, mixing until well blended. Add remaining ingredients, (not including potatoes) adding small amount of liquid if mixture is too dry. Pat meat mixture into 9"-10" ceramic quiche dish which has been sprayed with non-stick spray. Bake 35 40 minutes at 350 degrees. When meat loaf is done, top with mashed potatoes. Sprinkle with 3 Tbsp. Parmesan cheese and paprika. Return to oven for few minutes to melt cheese. Serve in wedges.

Yield: 6 wedges. 1 serving = 1 wedge

240 calories
23 grams carb.
20 grams protein

7 grams fat
50 mg cholesterol
287 mg sodium

1 1/2 starch/bread Exchanges
2 low-fat meat Exchanges

PIZZA ALA PATTI

This pizza is light on the cheese, but does tend to have a lot of salty items on it. You may adapt it to your needs.

Crust:
  1 cup warm water
  1 package dry yeast
  2 1/2 - 3 cups white flour
  1/2 cup whole wheat flour
  2 cloves garlic, minced
  1/8 tsp. salt

Topping:
  3/4 cup low sodium tomato chunks in puree
  spices to taste
      I use oregano, basil, garlic powder, pepper
  12 sun-dried tomato pieces chopped or sliced
  1/4 cup roasted red peppers
      If canned, dry them on paper towel.
  1/4 cup sliced black olives or kalamata olives
  2 tsp. capers
  2/3 cup crumbled feta cheese, or mozzarella

In medium bowl, combine water and yeast, stirring until yeast dissolves. Add 2 cups of flour, wheat flour, garlic, and salt. Mix well. Place dough on floured pastry cloth and knead for 3-5 minutes. Add flour as needed. Dough should not be sticky. Too much flour will make it stiff. When dough is smooth, place it in clean glass bowl which has been coated with 1/2 tsp. oil. Let dough rise 30 minutes. Roll out to size of pizza pan. I spray pan with non-stick coating then sprinkle 2 tsp. cornmeal over pan. Place dough on pan and press to shape of pan. Top with veggies, capers, and cheese. Be sure to use alternate items if the sodium content is too high. (For instance, mozzarella cheese is lower in sodium, fat, and calories than feta) Bake at 450 degrees for 10-15 minutes.

Yield: 8 very large pieces. 1 serving = 1 piece

217 calories   3 grams fat
40 grams carb.   8 mg cholesterol
8 grams protein   177 mg sodium

2 starch/bread Exchanges; 2 vegetable Exchanges

POLENTA PIE ITALIANO

Polenta is an Italian corn meal mush. I have used it as a crust in two versions of Polenta pizza or pie. Quite often hot peppers are added to it. I will leave that up to you.

>1 1/2 quarts water
>1 box (13 oz.) polenta (I use Fattorie & Pandea
>   instant polenta.) or corn meal
>   (for corn meal, use 1 1/4 corn meal to
>   2 1/2 cups water)
>1/2 tsp. salt
>1 16 oz. can or jar pizza sauce or 1 can
>   low sodium tomato sauce* + 1 tsp. basil
>1 tsp. garlic powder, 1/4 tsp. oregano
>2 Tbsp. dehydrated onion, chopped
>10 thin slices Canadian bacon or pepperoni (2 oz.)
>10 black olives, sliced
>10 mushrooms, sliced
>2/3 cup grated low-fat mozzarella cheese

In large saucepan, bring water to boil. Slowly, add polenta and salt, stirring constantly with wooden spoon so that mixture will not get lumpy. Cook over medium heat five minutes. (Polenta that is not instant will need to be cooked longer) Spray large pizza pan with non-stick coating spray. Spread hot polenta mixture onto tray with wooden spoon. This will make a 1/2" thick crust. Spread crust with layer pizza sauce followed by even layer of onion, Canadian bacon, black olives, and mushrooms. You may add other veggie favorites if you wish. Bake at 375 degrees for 20-30 minutes, until cheese is bubbly.

Yield: 8 large wedges. 1 serving = 1 wedge.

298 calories	11 grams fat
52 grams carb.	11 mg cholesterol
8 grams protein	486 mg sodium

3 starch/bread Exchanges
1 fat Exchange
* used in analysis

POLENTA PIE MEXICANO

This is a tasty and easy to prepare dish. It can be
as spicy as you wish to make it. It is high in fiber
and low in fat. A nice replacement for tamales or
chimichangas which contain lots of beef and cheese.

> 1 1/2 quarts water
> 1 box (13 oz.) polenta (I use Fattorie & Pandea instant
>   polenta.) or corn meal
> 1/2 tsp. salt
> 1 - 16 oz. can vegetarian refried beans
> 1 14.5 oz. can low sodium tomatoes, sliced or chopped
> 1 tsp. cumin
> 1 tsp. garlic powder
> 1 Tbsp. dehydrated onion, chopped
> 1 4 oz. can green chilies, diced
> 10 black olives, sliced
> 2/3 cup grated low-fat cheddar or jack cheese

In large saucepan, bring water to boil. Slowly, add polenta
and salt, stirring constantly with wooden spoon so that
mixture will not get lumpy. Cook over medium heat five
minutes. (Polenta that is not instant will need to be cooked
longer.) Spray large pizza pan with non-stick coating spray.
Spread hot polenta mixture onto tray with wooden spoon. This
will make a 1/2" thick crust. Spread crust with layer of
refried beans. In small bowl, combine tomatoes and spices.
(you may use canned tomatoes with Mexican seasonings ... if
you do this, do not add any additional spices) Pour tomato
mixture over crust. Sprinkle green chilies and olive slices
evenly over this mixture. Top with grated cheese. Bake at
375 degrees for 20-30 minutes, until cheese is bubbly.

Yield: 8 large wedges. 1 serving = 1 wedge.

260 calories	4 grams fat
46 grams carb.	7 mg cholesterol
10 grams protein	531 mg sodium

3 starch/bread Exchanges
1 fat Exchange

SHEPHERD'S PIE

I use the Hawaiian Hash as a base for this. You
can add any of your own favorite goodies. Since this
is topped with mashed potatoes, you may choose to
eliminate the potatoes in the hash.

Filling:
> 1 recipe Hawaiian Hash, using only 2 potatoes
> 1 recipe Healthy Cream Sauce
> 3 carrots, diced
> 2 celery stalks, diced
> 3 Tbsp. pimento, chopped

Topping:
> 4 potatoes (4 oz. ea.)
> > peeled, cut, boiled for mashing
> 1/3 cup skim milk
> 1/3 cup Parmesan cheese

In 2 quart casserole, combine filling ingredients. Cover
and refrigerate while preparing topping. Cook and mash
potatoes until smooth. Slowly, add milk and continue mashing
until fluffy. (If necessary, add a bit more milk; potatoes
should not be dry) Beat in half of the Parmesan. Spoon
potatoes over hash. Sprinkle with remaining cheese. Bake
at 350 degrees for 35-45 minutes, or until golden brown
and bubbly.

6 servings. 1 serving = 1 1/2 cup

296 calories	9 grams fat
40 grams carb.	28 mg cholesterol
14 grams protein	188 mg sodium

2 starch/bread Exchanges
1 low-fat meat Exchange
1 vegetable Exchange
1 fat Exchange

TAMALE PIE

A tasty cold weather meal. It is easy to make this dish meatless by mixing beans and wheat berry in place of the beef and turkey. Lots of ingredients, but easy.

1 cup cornmeal
2 cups water
1/8 tsp. salt
1/4 lb. extra lean ground beef
1/4 lb. ground turkey breast
1/2 onion, chopped
1 tsp. chili powder
1/2 tsp. cumin
1/4 tsp. oregano
1/4 tsp. garlic powder
1/8 tsp. cinnamon
1 cup kidney beans,rinsed, drained (optional)
1/2 cup cooked corn
1/4 cup green chilies, chopped
1/2 cup shredded low-fat cheddar or jack cheese
10 black olives, sliced

In small saucepan, combine first three ingredients and cook over medium heat until very thick. Pour mixture into large pie pan or quiche dish which has been sprayed with non-stick coating. Set aside. In large skillet, brown meats together. Stir in onion and spices, blending well. Add corn, chilies, and beans (if desired). Pour mixture into corn crust. Top with cheese and olives. Bake 30 minutes at 350 degrees. Serve with crisp green salad & corn or whole wheat tortillas.

Yield: 6 servings. 1 serving = 1/6 of recipe

(Analysis does not include beans.)
194 calories   5 grams fat
23 grams carb.   33 mg cholesterol
14 grams protein   208 mg sodium

1 1/2 starch/bread Exchanges
1 low-fat meat Exchange
1 fat Exchange

CHIPPED BEEF ALA BAKED POTATO

Today, there is a return to our comfort foods.
When I feel yukky and need a comfort food, I
always think of this one.

> 4 large baking potatoes, (5 oz. ea.) baked and hot
> 2 tsp. margarine
> 1 Tbsp. minced shallots
> 2 Tbsp. flour
> 1 3/4 cups low sodium chicken broth
> 1/4 cup non-fat milk
> 3 Tbsp. instant potato flakes
> 2 tsp. Dijon mustard
> 2 tsp. white wine
> 2 .5 oz. pkg. dried beef
> 1/2 cup non-fat yogurt
> fresh parsley

The sauce takes just a few minutes, so have potatoes
ready to serve. In large saucepan, saute shallots in
margarine until golden. Stir in flour and cook 1 minute.
Remove from heat and SLOWLY add 1/2 cup of broth, stirring
constantly. When smooth, add remaining broth, milk, and
potato flakes. Return to medium heat, stirring in mustard,
wine, and dried beef. Lower heat. Split hot potatoes open
in both directions. Fluff center of each potato with 2 Tbsp.
yogurt. Divide beef mixture in equal portions over potatoes.
Garnish with chopped fresh parsley.

4 servings. 1 serving = 1 potato
with 1/4 above sauce. (approx. 2/3 cup sauce per serving.)

240 calories	4 grams fat
42 grams carb.	15 mg cholesterol
10 grams protein	292 mg sodium

3 starch/bread Exchanges

REUBEN IN A WRAP

This is the craziest thing I have ever made. It is one of my test recipes for my childrens' cookbook. I had such fun doing it, especially since it received rave reviews, (thank you Shasta) so I am sharing it with you.

     1 pkg. (11 oz.) Pillsbury Crusty French Loaf
          refrigerated bread dough
          (others will work I am sure)
     1 - 15 oz. can sauerkraut, well drained
     2 tsp. caraway seed
     2 large slices Swiss cheese (3 oz. total)
     1 - 2 1/2 oz. pkg. chipped beef or pastrami

Un-roll bread dough on large heavy baking sheet which has been sprayed with non-stick coating. Down the center 1/3 of dough, pile the drained sauerkraut, leaving 1/2" of dough showing at each end. Sprinkle with caraway seed. Place cheese slices on top of sauerkraut and top with chipped beef slices. Overlap beef slices. Fold outside 1/3's of dough over filled center, pinching dough together at sides and ends. Bake 25-35 minutes at 325 degrees or until bread is golden brown.

Makes 6 servings. 1 serving = 1/6 of sandwich.
(approx. 2 1/2" slice.)

213 calories   6 grams fat
28 grams carb.   16 mg cholesterol
11 grams protein   911 mg sodium

2 Bread/Starch Exchange
1 Med. Fat Meat Exchange

FETA AND SPINACH FILLO (PHYLLO)

This is my off the wall version of Spanakopeta. It has the rich flavors without the rich fats. You won't miss the extra 1/2 lb. of butter!

> 1 tsp. oil
> 1 oz. prociutto, finely chopped, or
>   1/4 cup Canadian bacon, finely chopped
> 1/2 cup onion, chopped
> 2-10 oz. pkgs. frozen chopped spinach
> 2/3 cup low-fat ricotta cheese
> 1/3 cup non-fat yogurt
> 1/4 cup feta cheese, crumbled (if you do not
>   like feta, use Romano or Parmesan)
> 2 Tbsp. fresh mint
> 2 tsp. dill weed
> 1/2 tsp. nutmeg
> pepper
> 8 sheets fillo dough, thawed
> 3 tsp. melted margarine

In large skillet, over medium heat, combine oil, Canadian bacon, and onion. Saute mixture until onion is soft and golden. Add spinach and simmer 5 minutes over medium heat. Add ricotta cheese, yogurt, feta, and spices. Mix together well. Set aside. On pastry cloth, place 2 full sheets of fillo dough. Brush top piece lightly with melted margarine. Add 2 more pieces of fillo, again coating lightly with margarine. Spread half of spinach mixture along short side of dough. Spread spinach approx. 4" wide x length of dough. Roll dough in jelly roll fashion and pinch edges. Place on baking sheet. Cut 4 small slits in top of dough. Repeat process with remaining dough & spinach mixture. Bake at 375 degrees for 20-30 minutes or until gold & bubbly.

Makes 16 slices. 1 serving = 2 slices.

136 calories	6 grams fat
15 grams carb.	11 mg cholesterol
6 grams protein	261 mg sodium

1/2 starch/bread Exchange
1 vegetable Exchange
1 med. fat meat Exchange

HAM AND VEGGIE MEDLEY

This is one of those comfort foods. A real old fashioned combo that can use up a few leftovers if you desire. This version is heavy on veggies, light on fat.

1 - 8 oz. pkg. macaroni or bow tie noodles, cooked
1 recipe healthy cream sauce (from this book)
1 cup low-fat, low salt ham or dried beef
1 tsp. oil
1 medium onion, chopped
2 cups celery, sliced fine
1/2 cup green pepper, chopped
1 Tbsp. pimento, chopped
2 cloves garlic, crushed (optional)
1/2 cup grated cheese, (low-fat) or Parmesan
pepper
salt (optional)

In 3 quart casserole, combine cooked macaroni, cream sauce, and meat. Set aside. In large skillet, saute onion in oil until golden. Add celery and saute 2 minutes. Remove from heat and add to noodle mixture. Stir in green pepper, pimento, and garlic. Season. Top with grated cheese. Bake 30 minutes or until bubbly at 350 degrees. Green pepper and pimento can be left out if you are not thrilled about them, but they add color, texture, and very few calories.

Yield: 8 large servings. 1 serving = 1/8 recipe

198 calories	5 grams fat
27 grams carb.	15 mg cholesterol
11 grams protein	372 mg sodium

1 1/2 starch/bread Exchanges
1 vegetable Exchange
1 low-fat meat Exchange

HAWAIIAN HASH

Now don't expect the taste of the islands in this.
When I was in school in Hawaii, starving students
and surfers combined whatever was still in the
refrigerator to get this combination. I give the
credit to Pat and Bill. (wherever they are today.)
This is actually a great dish for a camp out. Of
course, if you know me, you know my idea of camping ...
the Hyatt with no room service ... sorryyyyy!

  2 tsp. oil
  4 large potatoes (5 oz. ea.) skin on, diced
  1 large onion, chopped
  1/2 lb. extra lean ground beef
  salt free spice combination to taste
  pepper to taste
  1 large green pepper, diced
  3-4 Tbsp. red wine vinegar or balsamic vinegar
  (don't laugh ... this makes the dish)

In one skillet, saute potatoes in 1 tsp. oil, until
slightly golden. Add water to cover them. Place lid
on skillet and steam potatoes until tender. In separate
skillet, saute onion in remaining oil. When tender, add
ground beef and brown well. Add cooked potatoes to meat
mixture. Stir in spices and green pepper. Cook until well
heated, keeping pepper crisp. Just before serving, add wine
vinegar. Top each serving with dollop of low-cal ketchup or
Tomato Herb (a great product by Wax Orchards ... fruit juice
sweetened chili-type sauce.) Serve with wheat rolls and
peanut butter.

Makes 4 servings. 1 serving = 1 1/2 cup.

295 calories	10 grams fat
40 grams carb.	35 mg cholesterol
15 grams protein	38 mg sodium

2 1/2 starch/bread Exchanges
1 low-fat meat Exchange
1 fat Exchange

AU GRATIN HASH BROWNS

This is a simple dish that is great for entertaining.
It is a great accompaniment with chicken or ham.

    1 (32 oz.) pkg. frozen hash brown potatoes
    1 cup healthy cream sauce
    1 1/2 cup non-fat yogurt
    1 cup low-fat cheddar cheese, shredded
    1/2 cup onion, finely chopped
    1/4 tsp. salt
    1 tsp. pepper
    1/2 tsp. paprika
    1 1/2 cups corn flake crumbs
        (If you have fruit juice sweetened
        corn flakes, make your own crumbs.)

In large bowl, combine ingredients in order, except corn
flake crumbs. Mix ingredients well. Spoon into 9" x 13"
glass baking dish, which has been sprayed with non-stick
coating. Bake at 350 degrees for 1 hour. Add corn flake
crumbs for last 15 minutes of baking only.

12 servings. 1 serving = 2/3 cup.

268 calories   11 grams fat
37 grams carb.   8 mg cholesterol
8 grams protein   286 mg sodium

2 1/2 starch/bread Exchanges
2 fat Exchanges

POTATO KUGEL

This is my rendition of a one of my favorites.
I like to make individual kugels in muffin tins.

> 3 Tbsp. finely chopped onion
> 1/2 tsp. oil
> 2 3/4 cup grated potato (about 3 - 5 oz. potatoes)
> 2 egg yolks
> 4 egg whites
> 1/3 cup matzo meal
> 3 Tbsp. oil
> 1/2 tsp. salt
> 1/4 tsp. pepper

In large skillet, saute onion in 1/2 tsp. oil until
transparent. In strainer or colander, rinse grated potato
thoroughly under cold water. In large bowl, combine
potatoes, onion, egg yolks, matzo meal, oil, and spices.
In separate bowl, beat egg whites until stiff, then fold
into potato mixture. Spray 9" x 13" glass baking dish with
non-stick coating. Pour mixture into dish and bake 45-55
minutes at 350 degrees. If using muffins tins, spray with
non-stick coating, and fill 18 tins with potato mixture
into dish and bake 45-55 minutes at 350 degrees. If using
muffin tins, spray with non-stick coating and fill 18 tins
with potato mixture. Bake at same temperature for 30-40
minutes. Makes 18 servings.

58 calories	3 grams fat
6 grams carb.	23 mg cholesterol
2 grams protein	87 mg sodium

1/2 starch/bread exchange
1 fat exchange

SPICED POTATO WEDGES

This is easy (one of my favorite words) and fast;
better yet, it is very good.

> 4 large (5 oz. each) red potatoes, scrubbed, dried,
>   parboiled (or partially cooked in microwave)
> 2 tsp. oil
> 1/2 cup dry bread crumbs
> 2 tsp. dill weed
> 2 tsp. garlic powder
> 1 tsp. dry mint
> 1/4 cup grated Parmesan cheese
> pepper to taste

Parboil potatoes until almost done, yet still firm. If
you wish, microwave whole potatoes on medium high for
approximately 8 minutes. Cut potatoes into 1" wedges and
place in 9" x 13" baking dish. Toss wedges with oil. In
medium bowl, combine remaining ingredients, blending well
with fork. Sprinkle crumb mixture over potatoes. Bake 30
minutes or until golden, at 375 degrees. Turn occasionally
with fork while baking.

Yield: 4 servings. 1 serving = 1/4 of recipe.

226 calories	5 grams fat
39 grams carb.	5 mg cholesterol
7 grams protein	215 mg sodium

2 starch/bread Exchanges
1 fat Exchange

GRAIN MEDLEY

Instead of just making rice to go with your dinner, you can increase the nutrients you receive and create a far more interesting meal by combining other grains with rice. Here is just one idea. You can go on from here to create your own. Some grains require more cooking time or more water, so you have to experiment a bit.

  2 tsp. Canola oil
  2 cloves garlic, crushed (optional)
  3 green onions, finely chopped
  1 cup dry mixed grains*
  2 1/2 cups liquid
       (water or broth/water combo low sodium)
  1/2 tsp. dill weed
  1/2 tsp. parsley

*Example: White, brown, or wild rice, bulgar, kasha, barley, pearl pasta (wash and drain all grains, except pasta)

In medium saucepan, saute garlic and onions in oil. Stir in grains and saute until grains have some color. Add liquid and spices, then stir over medium high heat until mixture bubbles. Lower heat and simmer mixture. Cover for 25 minut or until all grains are tender. Add water if necessary. Tasty and good for re-runs.

Yield: 6 servings. 1 serving = approx. 1/2 cup

117 calories   2 grams fat
22 grams carb.   0 mg cholesterol
3 grams protein   3 mg sodium

1 1/2 starch/bread Exchanges

ONION CASSEROLE

This is made with Walla Walla sweet onions. They are usually available in July and August. It will work with other onions, but the Walla Walla onions are very sweet. Jude Russell shared her recipe with me.

        7 1/2 cups chopped onion
        2 tsp. oil
        1 1/2 cup cooked rice
        2/3 cup low-fat ricotta or non-fat evaporated milk
        1/2 cup shredded low-fat cheddar or Parmesan
        1/4 tsp. salt, pepper to taste

In large skillet, saute onion until soft and golden. Add remaining ingredients and mix together well. Pour into 2 quart glass baking casserole or souffle dish. Bake at 350 degrees for 30 minutes.

6 servings. 1 serving = 2/3 cup.

219 calories   6 grams fat
33 grams carb.   15 mg cholesterol
10 grams protein   176 mg sodium

1 1/2 starch/bread Exchanges
2 vegetable Exchanges
1 fat Exchange

RICE DRESSING

A nice option for holiday times. I like to add lots of goodies to enhance the flavor and texture of this dressing. Great with chicken breasts or a holiday turkey.

2 tsp. oil
1/2 cup chopped scallions
1/4 cup finely chopped Canadian bacon
1/4 cup wild rice
1/4 cup orzo pasta
1/2 cup cooked wheat berry
1 cup white rice
2 1/4 cups low sodium chicken broth
2/3 cup sliced mushrooms
1 cup celery, chopped fine
1 cup water chestnuts, chopped
1/3 cup toasted almonds

In large skillet, saute scallions for 2 minutes. Stir in Canadian bacon, rices, pasta, and wheat berry. Saute until orzo becomes golden. Add liquid and cook over medium low heat until most of the water is absorbed. Stir in remaining ingredients and transfer to 9" x 13" glass baking dish. Salt and pepper to taste. Add small amount of poultry seasoning if desired. Bake 30 minutes at 350 degrees.

Makes 10 servings. 1 serving = 1/2 cup.

156 calories   4 grams fat
26 grams carb.   1 mg cholesterol
5 grams protein   54 mg sodium

1/2 Bread/Starch Exchange
1 Fat Exchange

STUFFING WITH STYLE

Most holiday stuffing contains lots of butter and fattening goodies. This is a light version of stuffing and you can vary it with additions of apple or a few chopped nuts. I add as many crunchies as possible without adding fatty foods.

      2 tsp. oil
      1 tsp. butter (this is just for flavor, you may
            choose to leave it out)
      2 large onions, finely chopped
      4 cups chopped celery
      1/4 cup finely chopped Canadian bacon or lean ham
      1 - 5 oz. can sliced water chestnuts, chopped
      1/2 cup toasted chopped almonds
      6-8 cups bread cubes, or stuffing mix*
      1 1/2 to 2 cups low sodium chicken broth

* If you use stuffing mix and are watching your salt, be sure to read what spices have been added. It is easier to control the spices if you do your own. Spices such as sage, garlic powder, pepper are great or use one of the salt free seasonings. (Mrs. Dash type)

In large skillet, combine oil, butter, onions, and celery. Saute over medium low heat until onion and celery are tender. In large bowl, combine other ingredients, except chicken broth. Add celery and onion mixture to other ingredients in bowl. Toss together. Add broth to your liking ... some people like it dry and some like it moist. Bake in large covered baking dish which has been sprayed with non-stick coating. (Do not bake in turkey) Bake 350 degrees 30-40 minutes.

Makes 14 servings. 1 serving = 1/2 cup.

112 calories	4 grams fat
16 grams carb.	2 mg cholesterol
4 grams protein	264 mg sodium

1 Bread/Starch Exchange
1 Fat Exchange

STUFFED PEPPERS

You may use green or red peppers. I prefer red because they are milder. This is a fun and colorful summer meal ... especially if you grow peppers in your garden. Thanks to Diana, my dear neighbor.

> 4 large red peppers, tops and seeds removed
> 2 tsp. oil
> 1 medium onion, chopped
> 1/2 cup celery, chopped
> 2 Tbsp. sunflower seeds
> 2 tsp. parsley
> 1/4 tsp. oregano
> 3/4 cup cooked rice, or rice/orzo combination*
> 2 egg whites, beaten
> 1/2 cup Parmesan cheese, shredded

Clean and prepare peppers. Set in 9" round glass quiche dish or baking dish. In large skillet over medium heat, saute onion and celery in oil for 3-5 minutes. Add sunflower seeds, spices, and rice. Remove from heat. Stir in beaten egg whites. Fold in cheese. (Reserve small amount of cheese to top each pepper) Bake at 350 degrees for 35-45 minutes or until thoroughly heated. Serve as main dish or as side dish with chicken breasts or fish.

4 servings. 1 serving = 1 pepper.

* See rice combination side dishes/grain medley

200 calories	9 grams fat
21 grams carb.	10 mg cholesterol
10 grams protein	278 mg sodium

1 starch/bread Exchange
1 vegetable Exchange
2 fat Exchanges

TSIMMES

Thank you again Roberta for sharing this recipe. I took some liberties with a few changes. Spicy holiday treat that is filled with healthy ingredients.

        2 yams, peeled, sliced very thin (2 cups)
        4 carrots, peeled, sliced very thin
        2 apples, cored, peeled, finely chopped
        1/2 cup chopped prunes
        1/3 cup currants
        1/3 cup toasted chopped almonds
        1/2 tsp. cinnamon
        4/2 tsp. ground cloves
        1/4 tsp. nutmeg
        1/4 tsp. salt
        2/3 cup orange juice
        2 Tbsp. toasted chopped almonds

Steam yam and carrot slices for 5 minutes. In large bowl combine all ingredients except juice and 2 Tbsp. almonds. Pour mixture into lightly oiled 2-3 quart glass baking or souffle dish. Pour orange juice over mixture and top with remaining almonds. Bake 30-40 minutes at 350 degrees.

Makes 8 servings. 1 serving = 2/3 cup.

170 calories	4 grams fat
33 grams carb.	0 mg cholesterol
3 grams protein	84 mg sodium

2 fruit Exchanges

1 fat Exchange

VEGETABLE MEDLEY

If I were to add more of anything to my daily diet, it would be vegetables. This was inspired by my mother, who believed in good nutrition before it was fashionable! She, also, used to take me on 3-4 mile walks as a toddler. I think I was the original race walker. Thanks MOM!

2 medium onions, chopped in 1" cubes
1 eggplant, peeled, diced in 1" cubes
3 zucchini, sliced
1 large red pepper, chopped in 1" cubes
2 large stalks, celery, in 1/2" slices
3 carrots, sliced very thin
1 cup orzo pasta (or other tiny pasta)
2 - 14.5 oz. cans low sodium tomato pieces or sauce
1 tsp. each oregano and basil
2 cloves garlic crushed
black pepper
2/3 cup shredded low-fat mozzarella or Parmesan

Spray 9" x 13" glass baking dish with non-stick spray. Layer vegetables in order. Sprinkle pasta over top of vegetables. In large bowl, combine tomatoes and spices. Pour this mixture over vegetables. Sprinkle cheese over top. Bake 1 hour at 350 degrees. Top each serving with dollop of non-fat yogurt, if desired.

Makes 10 servings. 1 serving = 1 1/4 cup.

108 calories	1 grams fat
9 grams carb.	5 mg cholesterol
5 grams protein	63 mg sodium

1/2 starch/bread Exchange
2 vegetable Exchanges

Desserts & Drinks

APRICOT CURRANT COOKIES

A great lunch sack treat. Kids love these tasty morsels!

1/4 cup margarine
1/4 cup non-fat plain yogurt
1/2 cup fruit sweetener
2 egg whites
1 cup flour
1 tsp. soda
1/4 tsp. salt
1 1/4 cup oatmeal
1/4 cup currants or golden raisins
3 Tbsp. chopped dried apricots
2 Tbsp. chopped toasted almonds

Place first three ingredients in large bowl. Microwave on high for 30 seconds, until margarine is melted. Beat in egg whites. In separate bowl, combine flour, soda, salt and stir into batter. Add remaining ingredients and combine well. Drop by teaspoonful onto Teflon coated cookie sheet. Bake 5-7 minutes at 325 degrees.

Makes 24 cookies. 1 serving = 1 cookie

79 calories	3 grams fat
12 grams carb.	0 mg cholesterol
2 grams protein	85 mg sodium

1 starch/bread Exchange

In the bread, muffin, and cookie recipes, you may substitute granulated fructose for the liquid fruit sweetener. You may also use frozen juice concentrate in place of the sweetener. (See page vi in front of book)

CRISPIE CRITTERS

This is a very simple cookie and everyone seems to like it ... and it isn't even chocolate!

> 1/4 cup margarine
> 1/2 cup fruit sweetener
> 1 egg white
> 1 cup flour
> 1/2 tsp. soda
> 1/4 tsp. salt
> 1 tsp. vanilla
> 2 cup crispy rice cereal

Combine margarine and fruit sweetener in large bowl and microwave on high for 30 seconds. Remove from microwave and beat egg white into mixture. In small bowl, combine flour, soda, and salt, then add to batter. Fold in vanilla and cereal. Drop teaspoonfuls onto Teflon coated cookie sheet. Bake 6 minutes at 325 degrees.

Yield: 24 cookies. 1 serving = 2 cookies

120 calories	4 grams fat
18 grams carb.	0 mg cholesterol
2 grams protein	184 mg sodium

1/2 starch/bread Exchange
1/2 fruit Exchange
1 fat Exchange

CHRISTMAS WREATH COOKIES

This was one of my favorites to make as a child because it was one of those hands-on cookies that actually looked like something when you were done!

> 2/3 cup margarine
> 1/2 cup fruit sweetener
> 2 tsp. fresh grated orange rind
> 1 egg
> 2 egg whites
> 3 1/2 cups flour
> 1 egg white
> 3 packets granulated fructose
> red & green sugar free gummy candies, (optional)
>   cut in small pieces

Combine margarine and fruit sweetener in large glass bowl and microwave on medium high for 1 minute or until margarine melts. Beat in orange rind, egg, and egg whites. Add flour, one third at a time, blending well after each addition. Add more flour, if necessary, when you are molding cookies. Chill dough for 1 hour. On floured pastry cloth, roll dough with your hands into sticks about 1/4" thick by 6" long. Form into wreath-like circle and twist or loop into single knot at top. Place on large heavy cookie sheet. After forming cookies, beat egg white and fructose together until stiff. With pastry brush, spread each wreath with light coating of meringue. Bake at 375 degrees until golden, 5-8 minutes. Cool cookies slightly and add pieces of red and green gummy candies for holly.

Makes about 60 cookies. 1 serving = 2 cookies

106 calories	4 grams fat
14 grams carb.	8 mg cholesterol
2 grams protein	54 mg sodium

1 starch/bread Exchange
1 fat Exchange

FRUIT OATIES

This is another bar cookie! I like it because it is a high
energy goodie. It is worth your while to seek out dried
cranberries. They are fairly new on the market, so they
may be hard to find ... best if unsweetened or sweetened
with fructose. You may substitute dried bing cherries or
currants.

> 1/2 cup fruit sweetener
> 1/4 cup oil
> 1 egg white
> 1 tsp. vanilla
> 1 tsp. orange or lemon flavoring
> 3/4 cup flour
> 1/2 cup oat bran
> 1 tsp. soda
> 1/8 tsp. salt (optional)
> 1 cup granola, low-fat, fruit sweetened
> 1/3 cup dried cranberries, sweetened with fructose

In large bowl, combine first five ingredients, stirring
until well blended. In a separate bowl, mix dry ingredients
together. Add dry mixture to wet batter and stir 1-2 minutes.
Pour batter into 9" x 9" square pan which has been sprayed
with non-stick spray. Bake 10-15 minutes at 325 degrees.
These bars will be moist and store well. Do not over-bake
or they will be dry.

Yield: 16 bars. 1 serving = 1 bar

111 calories	4 grams fat
19 grams carb.	0 mg cholesterol
2 grams protein	60 mg sodium

1 starch/bread Exchange
1 fat Exchange

MOIST OATMEAL COOKIES

This is for Shirley Schnoll of Houston ... her husband
wanted a moist oatmeal cookie. The chopped raisins add
to the moistness.

  1/2 cup oil
  3/4 cup of fruit sweetener
  1 egg
  1 egg white
  2 Tbsp. applesauce, unsweetened
  1/2 cup golden raisins, chopped
  1 1/2 cups flour
  1 tsp. baking soda
  1/4 tsp. salt
  1 tsp. cinnamon
  1/4 tsp. cloves
  1 1/2 cups oatmeal

In large bowl, combine oil and fruit sweetener. When well
blended, beat in egg, egg white, applesauce, and chopped
raisins. In separate bowl, combine dry ingredients, mixing
well. Add dry ingredients to wet mixture, about 1/3 at a
time, stirring well after each addition. Drop spoonfuls of
cookie dough onto baking sheet which has been sprayed with
non-stick spray. Flatten cookies with fork. (dough is gooey)
Bake at 325 degrees 5-7 minutes. Makes 24 cookies.

1 serving = 1 cookie

122 calories   5 grams fat
17 grams carb.   9 mg cholesterol
2 grams protein   62 mg sodium

1 starch/bread Exchange
1 fat Exchange

RUGULACH

I love these in their original form, but I wanted a guilt
free version, so I have again used fruit sweetened preserves
and taken out lots of the fat calories. Thank you Roberta
Hershon for your contribution on this and other yummy recipe

- 1/4 cup butter, softened, (or margarine)
- 1/2 cup low-fat ricotta cheese
- 1/2 cup low-fat cottage cheese
- 1/4 cup non-fat plain yogurt
- 2 cups flour
- 1/8 tsp. salt
- 3 tsp. oil or melted margarine
- 9 Tbsp. fruit sweetened apricot preserves
     or fruit sweetener, if you prefer
- 3 tsp. cinnamon
- 9 Tbsp. finely chopped almonds
- 9 Tbsp. currants

In large bowl, cream together first four ingredients.
Stir in flour and salt. Divide dough in three sections.
On floured pastry cloth, roll one section into 12" circle.
Brush with 1 tsp. melted margarine. Spread with 3 Tbsp.
apricot preserves. Sprinkle with 1 tsp. cinnamon, 3 Tbsp.
almonds, and 3 Tbsp. currants. Keep currants and nuts
towards outside edge so they don't fall out when baking.
Cut into 12 wedges and roll up from outside toward center.
Place on baking sheet. Repeat with other 2 pieces of dough.
Brush with beaten egg white if desired. Bake at 350 degrees
for 12 minutes or until lightly browned.

Yield: 36 cookies. Serving = 1 piece

72 calories	3 grams fat
9 grams carb.	5 mg cholesterol
2 grams protein	37 mg sodium

1/2 starch/bread Exchange
1 fat Exchange

SKI DAY COOKIES

A silly name ... but when I am skiing I like to have a couple of these tucked in an accessible spot for a quick energy boost.

> 1/2 cup fruit sweetener
> 1/2 cup peanut butter
> 1 egg white
> 3 Tbsp. water
> 1/8 tsp. salt
> 2/3 cup flour
> 1/2 cup oat bran
> 1 cup low-fat fruit sweetened granola
> 1/3 cup currants

In a medium size bowl, combine fruit sweetener and peanut butter, stirring until well blended. Beat in egg white and water. In separate bowl, combine salt, flour, and oat bran. Add dry ingredients to wet mixture. Stir in granola and currants. (Another fun option is using 1/4 cup dried fruit sweetened cranberries in place of currants.) This is a new product in our area. Drop by teaspoonfuls onto cookie sheet which has been sprayed with non-stick coating. Flatten cookies with fork. Bake at 325 degrees for 6-8 minutes or until golden. Watch them so they don't over-bake.

Makes 24 cookies. 1 serving = 1 cookie

83 calories	3 grams fat
13 grams carb.	0 mg cholesterol
3 grams protein	40 mg sodium

1 starch/bread Exchange
1/2 fat Exchange

SPICE HOLIDAY COOKIES

A spicy cookie that can be rolled into your favorite shapes. You can add a tiny bit of food coloring to granulated fructose and sprinkle it on the baked cookie. If you sprinkle it on before baking, it will be like a glaze.

 1 tsp. butter, melted
 3 Tbsp. margarine, melted
 3/4 cup fruit sweetener
 1 egg
 1 egg white
 1/2 tsp. lemon extract
 2 1/3 cups sifted flour
 2 tsp. baking powder
 1/4 tsp. salt
 1 tsp. cinnamon
 1/4 tsp. nutmeg
 1/3 cup finely chopped pecans or almonds

Combine first three ingredients and blend well. Beat in egg, egg white, and lemon extract. In separate bowl, combine dry ingredients, except nuts. One third at a time, add dry mixture to wet mixture, stirring well after each addition. Add nuts. Roll dough out 1/4 at a time on lightly floured pastry cloth to 1/16" thick. Cut out your favorite shapes. With spatula, place on cookie sheet which has been sprayed with non-stick coating. Decorate as desired. Bake at 350 degrees for only 4-6 minutes. Watch these carefully! Bake until lightly golden.

Yield: 36 cookies. 1 serving = 2 cookies

120 calories	4 grams fat
19 grams carb.	12 mg cholesterol
3 grams protein	98 mg sodium

1 starch/bread Exchange
1 fat Exchange

CHEESECAKE BARS

It was love at first bite when my neighbor, Karen Johnson, served these in her home. This is my fruit sweetened, low-fat adaptation of her wonderful recipe.

> 1/3 cup margarine
> 1/4 cup fruit sweetener
> 2 cups flour
> 1/2 cup chopped pecans
> 1 - 8 oz. package light (low-fat) cream cheese
> 1/3 cup fruit sweetener
> 1/2 cup low-fat ricotta cheese
> 2 egg whites
> 2 Tbsp. fresh lemon juice
> 1 tsp. vanilla

Preheat oven to 325 degrees. In medium bowl, blend together with fork the first four ingredients. When well combined and crumbly, scoop about half of mixture into 9" x 13" pan which has been sprayed with non-stick coating. Press this mixture into bottom of pan for crust. Bake this mixture for about 4 minutes. Set aside remaining crumbly mixture. In large bowl, beat (with electric mixer) cream cheese until smooth. Continue beating and, slowly, add fruit sweetener. When mixture is well blended, add ricotta and continue beating. Add remaining ingredients and, when smooth, pour it on top of crust. Sprinkle remaining crumb mixture over cheese mixture and return to oven for 16-20 minutes. Cool thoroughly. Chill overnight.

Yield: 48 bars. 1 serving = 1 bar

60 calories	3 grams fat
7 grams carb.	3 mg cholesterol
2 grams protein	47 mg sodium

1/2 fruit Exchange
1 fat Exchange

HONEY CAKE (WITHOUT THE HONEY)

One of the sweet treats often featured at Rosh Hashanah.
A wish for a sweet and joy filled year to come. I have cut
way down on the number of egg yolks normally used and it
is still a sweet treat!

    4 egg yolks
    3/4 cup fruit sweetener
    1/4 cup oil
    1 1/4 cup cake flour
    1 Tbsp. potato starch
    1 tsp. cinnamon
    1 tsp. allspice
    1/4 tsp. nutmeg
    1/4 tsp. salt
    1/3 cup hazelnuts, finely chopped, toasted,
    8 egg whites, stiffly beaten

In large bowl, beat together egg yolks, fruit sweetener,
and oil. Stir in dry ingredients, including hazelnuts. Fold
stiffly beaten egg whites into batter. Pour into 9" spring-
form pan which has been sprayed with non-stick coating. Bak
at 350 degrees for 45-55 minutes or until center springs up
when lightly touched.

Yield: 16 pieces. 1 serving = 1 piece

132 calories   6 grams fat
15 grams carb.   53 mg cholesterol
4 grams protein   63 mg sodium

1 starch/bread Exchange
1 fat Exchange

APPLE BUTTER DESSERT CAKE

I have had numerous requests for an apple butter cake.
This one is especially for Betsy of Wax Orchards because
she makes such great apple butter.

> 2/3 cup fruit sweetened apple butter
> 1/4 cup fruit sweetener
> 2 Tbsp. Canola oil
> 3 egg whites, beaten
> 3/4 cup non-fat plain yogurt
> 2 cups flour
> 1 1/2 tsp. baking powder
> 1/4 tsp. baking soda
> 1/8 tsp. salt
> 1/2 tsp. nutmeg
> 1 tsp. vanilla

Topping:
> 3 Tbsp. fruit sweetener
> 1/2 cup instant potato flakes
> 1 tsp. cinnamon
> 1/4 tsp. nutmeg
> 3 Tbsp. currants
> 3 Tbsp. chopped nuts

Preheat oven to 350 degrees. In a large bowl, mix together
the first three ingredients. Add the egg whites and yogurt,
blending until smooth. In a medium bowl, stir together all
of the dry ingredients. Gradually add flour mixture to
batter, stirring well after each addition. Blend in vanilla
and pour mixture into 8" round spring form pan which has
been sprayed with non-stick spray. In a small bowl, combine
topping ingredients and sprinkle over batter. Bake 30-45
minutes. If using 9" x 13" pan, bake 20 minutes or until
set in center.

Makes 20 servings. 1 serving = 1 piece

100 calories	2 grams fat
19 grams carb.	0 mg cholesterol
3 grams protein	62 mg sodium

1/2 starch/bread Exchange
1 fruit Exchange

NEW ORLEANS SPICE CAKE

This is a strange combination of ingredients, but it works for a moist, heavy, spicy, chocolate dessert. Great topped with a light drizzle of hot fudge or chocolate drizzle.

> 2/3 cup fruit sweetener
> 3 Tbsp. imported Dutch cocoa (regular will work)
> 1/4 cup strong coffee
> 2 Tbsp. oil
> 1/4 cup orange juice
> 1 egg
> 4 egg whites
> 2 cups flour
> 2 tsp. baking powder
> 1/8 tsp. salt
> 1 tsp. cinnamon
> 1/2 tsp. cloves
> 14 tsp. nutmeg
> 1/4 tsp. anise
> 1/3 cup finely chopped prunes (optional)

In large bowl, combine first five ingredients, beating well. Beat in egg and egg whites until mixture is fluffy. In separate bowl, combine remaining ingredients (except prunes), blending well. Add dry ingredients to wet mixture and beat two minutes. (If using prunes, add at this point.) Pour batter into 9" x 13" cake pan (or 9" round spring-form) which has been sprayed with non-stick spray. Bake at 325 degrees for 20-30 minutes or until cake springs back when lightly touched. Increase baking time slightly in spring-form pan.

Yield: 16 pieces. 1 serving = 1 piece

116 calories	2 grams fat
20 grams carb.	13 mg cholesterol
3 grams protein	76 mg sodium

1 starch/bread Exchange
1/2 fruit Exchange

PENNSYLVANIA DUTCH CAKE

This is my version of a recipe given to me years ago by my dear friend, Dena Rapp, of St. Petersburg, Florida.

    2 1/4 cup flour
    1 tsp. baking powder
    1/4 tsp. baking soda
    1/4 tsp. salt
    1/2 cup fruit sweetener
    1/2 cup non-fat plain yogurt
    1 Tbsp. butter, melted
    2 Tbsp. margarine, melted
    2/3 non-fat milk
    1 tsp. cinnamon
    3 Tbsp. fruit sweetener

In medium bowl, combine first four ingredients, blending well. In large bowl, mix fruit sweetener and yogurt. Melt butter and margarine together; add 1/3 of this mixture to wet mixture. Add milk and flour mixture alternately to batter, stirring well after each addition. When well combined, pour mixture into 9" square pan which has been sprayed with non-stick spray. To remaining margarine, add cinnamon and 3 Tbsp. fruit sweetener. Blend well and spoon over batter, pressing it slightly into batter so it will not flow to edges. Bake 20-25 minutes at 325 degrees or until cake is set.

Yield: 16 squares. 1 serving = 1 square

118 calories	2 grams fat
21 grams carb.	3 mg cholesterol
3 grams protein	101 mg sodium

1 starch/bread Exchange
1/2 fruit Exchange

BAKLAVA

This is a version of Betsy Sestrap's fruit sweetened Baklava. It is very rich and you will never know you are missing the calories!

> 1/3 cup margarine, melted
> 16 sheets fillo (phyllo) dough
> 1 1/4 cup apple butter, fruit juice sweetened
> 1/3 - 1/2 cup fruit sweetener
> 1/2 cup toasted chopped almonds

You have to spread the margarine thin on the layers of phyllo. Layer phyllo (4 sheets on bottom layer) in 11" x 17" jelly roll pan which has been sprayed with non stick coating. Brush entire surface with melted margarine with pastry brush. Spread apple butter over entire surface evenly. Repeat process, 3 sheets at a time, brushing top sheet with margarine until you have 5 layers. None of the apple butter is needed for top layer. Pour fruit sweetener over top layer, coating entire surface. Sprinkle almonds over entire surface. Cut into diamond shapes before baking. Bake at 350 degrees for 15. Turn heat to 400 degrees. Bake 5-10 minute more.

Yield: 36 pieces. 1 serving = 1 piece

65 calories	3 grams fat
91 grams carb.	tr mg cholesterol
tr grams protein	55 mg sodium

2/3 fruit Exchange
1/2 fat Exchange

CUSTARD

This is an answer to many requests for a fruit sweetened custard. I have reduced the egg yolks to alleviate some of the cholesterol. This has a tasty topping.

    2 whole eggs
    2 egg whites
    1/4 cup fruit sweetener
    1 3/4 cup skim milk
    1 tsp. vanilla

Topping: 1 Tbsp. fruit sweetener + 1 tsp. cinnamon

Using electric mixer (on low) or whisk, lightly beat eggs and egg whites together until very well blended. Slowly, beat in remaining ingredients. Pour custard into 4 custard cups or ramekins. Place custard cups in large shallow baking dish. Pour hot water into baking dish until 1" deep. Bake at 325 degrees for 35-40 minutes or until set. Just before serving, drizzle each custard with a small amount of topping.

Yield: 4 servings 1 serving = 1 custard cup

136 calories   3 grams fat
18 grams carb.   108 mg cholesterol
9 grams protein   114 mg sodium

1 fruit Exchange
1 low-fat milk Exchange

CHOCOLATE DECADENCE

This recipe comes from my dear friend, accomplished chef, and publicist, Roberta Hershon. She has managed to create a lower fat chocoholics dream: have your cake and eat it, too. Leftovers (if there are any) will keep up to a week in the refrigerator.

> 4 Tbsp. imported Dutch cocoa
> 1/2 cup fruit sweetened fudge topping
> 1/2 cup fruit sweetener
> 1 stick margarine, cut into small chunks.
> 1 Tbsp. butter
> 1 tsp. vanilla or orange extract
> 4 eggs, slightly beaten

Topping:
> 3 oz. light cream cheese
> 1 Tbsp. vanilla
> 1 Tbsp. fruit sweetener
> skim milk to thin

Position rack to center of oven. Preheat oven to 350 degrees. Spray 9" cake pan with non-stick spray. Line pan with circle of parchment; spray with non-stick spray. Combine first four ingredients in food processor, fitted with steel blade. Turn on machine and let run until all ingredients are well blended. With machine running, add vanilla, then eggs (one at a time). When batter is smooth, turn off machine and scrape batter into prepared pan. Tap pan on counter to release air bubbles.

Topping:
Combine all ingredients, except milk, in medium bowl. Beat until smooth with electric mixer. Thin with small amount of milk to make topping the consistency of pudding. Place spoonfuls of topping on batter randomly and swirl with knife. Bake in water bath for 30 minutes or until cake is set. Remove from oven; cool 10 minutes. Tip cake out on cookie sheet, then back up onto plate. (so that cream cheese design shows) Let cool. When cool, cover and store in refrigerator.

20 servings. 1 serving = 1 piece
120 calories   7 grams fat
13 grams carb.   46 mg cholesterol
2 grams protein   97 mg sodium
1 fruit Exchange; 1 fat Exchange

CHOCOLATE RASPBERRY CHEESECAKE

This is a great holiday treat. Though it tastes rich, it is light on fat. For Christmas, garnish with crushed candy canes. (They do come sugar free)

        1 cup finely crushed pretzels
        2 Tbsp. fruit sweetener
        1 - 8 oz. pkg. light cream cheese, softened
        1 cup low-fat cottage cheese
        2/3 cup fruit sweetener
        1/4 cup imported dutch cocoa
        1 egg white (use jumbo egg white)
        1 tsp. vanilla
        1/3 cup raspberry preserves (fruit juice sweetened)

Combine crushed pretzels and 2 Tbsp. fruit sweetener in small bowl. Sprinkle mixture into bottom of 8" spring-form pan. Set aside. In food processor or large bowl, combine cream cheese and cottage cheese. Using processor or electric beaters, blend until very smooth. Add sweetener and cocoa, processing until well blended. Add remaining ingredients. When mixture is smooth, pour over pretzel crust. Bake at 300 degrees for 45-55 minutes or until well set in center. (it can set up quickly) Cool before serving.

12 servings. 1 serving = 1 piece

133 calories	4 grams fat
21 grams carb.	8 mg cholesterol
5 grams protein	271 mg sodium

1 fruit Exchange
1/2 starch/bread Exchange
1 fat Exchange

LAYERED LEMON CHEESECAKE

This may sound crazy, but it is good. Inspired by Kara of Vancouver who wanted a crumb crust with no refined sugar.

Crust:
- 1 cup tiny pretzels
- 10 whole almonds
- 2 Tbsp. fruit sweetener or fruit juice concentrate

Filling:
- 1 cup water
- 3 Tbsp. cornstarch
- 2/3 cup fruit sweetener
- 1 egg yolk
- 1/4 cup lemon juice
- 4 oz. low-fat or light cream cheese, softened
- 4 oz. low-fat ricotta cheese
- 2 tsp. fruit sweetener

Preheat oven to 350 degrees. In food processor or chopper, combine pretzels and almonds and chop for 20 seconds. In bowl, combine this mixture with fruit sweetener, blend, then press into bottom of 8" spring-form pan. Set aside. In medium size saucepan, combine 1/4 cup water and cornstarch; stir until smooth. Slowly, add remaining water and 2/3 cup fruit sweetener; continue stirring. Place pan over medium heat, stirring constantly until mixture is very thick and bubbly. (takes about 8 minutes) Remove from heat, Pour a small amount of mixture into bowl with beaten egg yolk. When blended, pour entire mixture back into saucepan. Place again over medium heat, continue stirring and add lemon juice. Cook for 2-3 minutes. Remove pudding from heat and cool. In medium bowl, using electric mixer, cream together last three ingredients. When pudding is cool, pour half of it over crust. Beat remaining pudding into cream cheese mixture. Pour cheese mixture over pudding and bake 20 min. or until set. Cool. Chill in refrigerator before serving.

8 servings. 1 serving = 1 piece

173 calories	6 grams fat
26 grams carb.	36 mg cholesterol
4 grams protein	170 mg sodium

1 starch/bread Exchange; 1 fruit Exchange; 1 fat Exchange

PEANUT BUTTER TRUFFLE PIE

This is a recipe requested by Betsy of Wax Orchards.
She sent me a version and asked me to remove fat,
refined sugar, and calories. Here it is!

>   1 cup crushed pretzels
>   2 Tbsp. fruit sweetener
>   1/4 cup margarine, softened
>   1 Tbsp. butter, softened
>   4 oz. light cream cheese
>   1/2 cup low-fat ricotta cheese
>   3 Tbsp. fruit sweetener
>   1/2 cup peanut butter fudge topping (fruit juice sweetened)
>   2 egg whites
>   1 tsp. vanilla

Combine pretzels and 2 Tbsp. fruit sweetener and press
into bottom of 8" or 9" pie pan. In large bowl, combine
margarine, butter, cream cheese, and ricotta. With electric
mixer, beat until smooth. Add fruit sweetener and fudge
topping, blending well. Beat in egg whites and vanilla.
Pour mixture over pretzel crust. Bake 20 minutes or until
firm, at 325 degrees. Cool thoroughly before serving.

Makes 8 servings. 1 serving = 1 piece

231 calories   10 grams fat
30 grams carb.   14 mg cholesterol
5 grams protein   317 mg sodium

1 starch/bread Exchange
1 fruit Exchange
2 fat Exchanges

PEACH CRUNCH

This is a recipe I love! It is the easiest recipe in the
book. I first made it using DEBBIE'S FAMOUS GRANOLA. Her
granola is great. I use the original flavor with peaches.
For blueberry crunch, I use Country Berry flavor. If using
another brand of low-fat fruit juice sweetened granola, add
2 tsp. melted margarine to granola.

> 6 fresh peaches, peeled and sliced
> 3 Tbsp. fruit juice sweetener or frozen juice
>   concentrate
> 1 tsp. vanilla
> 1 tsp. cinnamon
> 1 1/2 cups fruit juice sweetened, low-fat granola

In large bowl, combine peaches, fruit sweetener, vanilla,
and cinnamon. Mix well. Pour this mixture into a 9" square
glass baking dish which has been sprayed with non-stick
spray. Sprinkle granola evenly over fruit. Bake at 325
degrees for 25 minutes or until golden and bubbly. Serve
warm or cold. Yield: 9 servings. To make blueberry crunch,
replace peaches with 3 cups blueberries.

1 serving = 1 square

105 calories   2 grams fat
21 grams carb.   0 mg cholesterol
3 grams protein   7 mg sodium

1 fruit Exchange
1/2 starch/bread Exchange

BLUEBERRY STRUDEL

A nice treat on the 4th of July: one cherry strudel and
one blueberry strudel. Tasty and colorful! This formula
will work with other fruits as well. A cherry strudel will
probably require a total of 1/3 cup fruit sweetener.

>   1 cup fresh or frozen blueberries
>   4 Tbsp. fruit sweetener
>   or fruit sweetened blueberry preserves
>   4 Tbsp. dry bread crumbs
>   1/2 tsp. almond extract
>   1/4 cup toasted chopped almonds
>   4 sheets fillo (or phyllo) dough
>   2 Tbsp. margarine or butter, melted

In large bowl, combine blueberries, fruit sweetener, bread
crumbs, almond extract, and almonds. Mix well and set aside.
On large heavy baking sheet, place two full sheets of fillo
dough. Brush top sheet lightly with melted margarine. Add
two more sheets of fillo and, again, spread with margarine.
Spread berry mixture evenly along short side of dough.
Starting from this end, fold dough around filling as for
a jelly roll. Place seam side down on cookie sheet. Brush
top lightly with remaining margarine. Turn ends under, if
possible. Bake at 375 degrees 20-25 minutes or until golden.

Yield: 8 slices. 1 serving = 1 slice

116 calories   6 grams fat
15 grams carb.   0 mg cholesterol
2 grams protein   98 mg sodium

1 fruit Exchange
1 fat Exchange

APPLE STRUDEL

My strudel recipes are light, yet rich tasting. The most important thing to do is make the butter or margarine stretch. Think thin. This is one of those recipes where I personally like to use part butter. (Exchange uses margarine.)

>1 cup chopped apple (1 - 1 1/2 large apple)
>3 Tbsp. fruit sweetener
>   or fruit sweetened apple butter
>4 Tbsp. dry bread crumbs
>zest of one orange
>3 Tbsp. currants
>cinnamon to taste
>4 sheets fillo (or phyllo) dough
>2 Tbsp. margarine or butter, melted

In large bowl, combine apple, fruit sweetener, bread crumbs, orange zest, currants, and cinnamon. Mix well and set aside. On large heavy baking sheet, place two full sheets of fillo dough. Brush top sheet lightly with melted margarine. Add two more sheets of fillo and, again, spread with margarine. Spread apple mixture evenly along short side of dough. Starting from this end, fold dough around filling as for a jelly roll. Place seam side down on cookie sheet. Brush top lightly with remaining margarine. Turn ends under, if possible. Bake at 375 degrees 20-25 minutes or until golden.

Yield: 8 slices. 1 serving = 1 slice

102 calories	4 grams fat
17 grams carb.	0 mg cholesterol
1 grams protein	97 mg sodium

1 fruit Exchange
1 fat Exchange

APPLE KUGEL (PUDDING)

This is a spicy little addition to any meal. I like
using Granny Smith apples best ... I grate them in my
food processor with the skin on.

    1/2 cup fruit sweetener or apple juice concentrate
    2 egg yolks
    4 large Granny Smith apples, cored, and grated
          with skin on
    1/2 cup matzo meal or bread crumbs
    1 tsp. cinnamon
    1 tsp. lemon zest
    4 egg whites
    1/2 cup toasted chopped almonds

In large bowl, beat together fruit sweetener and egg yolks.
Stir in grated apples. Add matzo meal, cinnamon, and lemon
zest. In separate bowl, beat egg whites until stiff. Gently
fold egg whites into apple mixture. Pour mixture into 2-3
quart glass souffle or baking dish which has been sprayed
with non-stick coating. Sprinkle almonds evenly over top of
pudding. Bake 35-45 minutes at 325 degrees.

Yield: 6 cups. 1 serving = 1/2 cup

117 calories   4 grams fat
17 grams carb.   35 mg cholesterol
3 grams protein   51 mg sodium

1 starch/bread Exchange
1 fat Exchange

NOODLE KUGEL

This is a rendition of a wonderful recipe from
Roberta Hershon. She is such a great chef.

> 8 oz. egg noodles
> 1 cup low-fat cottage cheese
> 1 cup non-fat plain yogurt
> 4 oz. low-fat neufchatel
> > or philly light cream cheese, softened
> 1 egg white
> 1/4 cup non-fat milk
> 1 Tbsp. butter
> 1 Tbsp. margarine
> 1/3 cup fruit sweetened apricot or peach preserves
> 1/2 tsp. cinnamon
> 1/2 vanilla
> 1/3 cup golden raisins

Topping:
> 3/4 cup corn flakes crumbs
> 1/2 tsp. cinnamon

Cook noodles per package directions and drain. Set aside.
In large bowl, cream together cottage cheese, yogurt, and
cream cheese. When well blended, add egg white, milk,
butter, and margarine. Mix until smooth. Stir in remaining
ingredients. Add noodles, stirring thoroughly. Spread
mixture in 9" square baking dish, which has been sprayed
with non-stick coating. Combine corn flake crumbs with
cinnamon, and sprinkle over top of noodle mixture. Bake
20-30 minutes at 350 degrees.

Makes 9 servings. 1 serving = 3" x 3" square.

247 calories	6 grams fat
39 grams carb.	35 mg cholesterol
10 grams protein	327 mg sodium

2 starch/bread Exchanges
1/2 non-fat milk Exchange
1 fat Exchange

LEMON BLUEBERRY TART

The French version of this yummy dessert calls for a total of 1 cup of butter. This version has 2 Tbsp. of butter and 1/4 as much oil!

- 1 cup flour
- 1/4 cup instant mashed potato flakes
- 3 Tbsp. fruit sweetener
- 2 Tbsp. oil
- 1 Tbsp. butter
- 1 egg white
- 1/3 cup water
- 3 Tbsp. cornstarch
- 2/3 cup fruit sweetener
- 1/2 cup lemon juice
- 2 tsp. butter
- 1 egg
- 1 3/4 cup blueberries
- 1 Tbsp. fruit sweetener

In medium bowl, combine flour, potato flakes, fruit sweetener, butter, and oil. Stir with fork until well combined. Blend in egg white. Work with fingers until dough holds together. Press into 8" or 9" tart pan. Bake at 300 degrees for 10 minutes until golden. Cool. In top of double boiler, combine water and cornstarch, stirring until smooth. Add fruit sweetener and lemon juice. Place over medium heat, stirring constantly, until mixture is thick and smooth. Add butter, and stir until melted. Remove from heat. In small bowl, beat egg. Stir small amount of lemon mixture into egg; blend and pour egg mixture back into lemon mixture. Continue to stir, and heat for one additional minute. Remove from heat and cool well. When cool pour lemon mixture over crust. Let set. (Chill if desired.) Combine berries and sweetener. Spoon over tart when ready to serve.

Cut in 12 wedges. 1 serving = 1 wedge

147 calories	4 grams fat
26 grams carb.	20 mg cholesterol
2 grams protein	22 mg sodium

1 fruit Exchange
1 starch/bread Exchange
1 fat Exchange

FRENCH FRUIT TART

Follow the recipe for Lemon Blueberry Tart, except for the blueberry topping. In center of tart place a small circle of blueberries; followed by a row of peeled, sliced kiwi fruit; followed by a row of sliced fresh strawberries with an outside row of sliced grapes.

Yield: 12 slices. 1 serving = 1 slice

146 calories   4 grams fat
26 grams carb.   20 mg cholesterol
2 grams protein   22 mg sodium

1 fruit Exchange
1/2 starch/bread Exchange
1 fat Exchange

TOPPINGS

When you make pies and cobblers, it is nice to have a
variety of possible toppings. Here are some that I use.

GRANOLA TOPPING

1 1/3 cups Debbies Famous Granola

That's it! Debbie's Granola has no added fat, but it is
so fabulous that you just sprinkle it over your favorite
fruit cobbler combination. If using another low-fat fruit
sweetened granola, add 3 tsp. margarine or oil plus 2 Tbsp.
fruit juice concentrate to granola.

Total topping = 1 1/2 cups. 1 serving = 1/8 of recipe
(Debbie's granola)

65 calories	2 grams fat
11 grams carb.	0 mg cholesterol
3 grams protein	7 mg sodium

3/4/ starch/bread Exchange
1/2 fat Exchange

POTATO FLAKE TOPPING

     1 1/4 cup instant potato flakes
     3 Tbsp. fruit sweetener
     2 Tbsp. finely chopped almonds

Combine above ingredients in medium bowl. Blend together
well with fork. Sprinkle over fruit. Sufficient for 8" or
9" pan.

1 serving = 1/8 of recipe

56 calories   1 grams fat
11 grams carb.   0 mg cholesterol
1 grams protein   9 mg sodium

3/4 starch/bread Exchange

MATZO MEAL TOPPING

     1 cup matzo meal
     3 Tbsp. margarine, melted
     1/3 cup fruit sweetener or juice concentrate
     1 tsp. nutmeg
     1/2 tsp. cinnamon

Combine above ingredients in medium bowl. Blend with
fork until crumbly and well combined. Sprinkle over
fruit mixture of choice.

1 serving = 1/8 of recipe

128 calories   5 grams fat
20 grams carb.   0 mg cholesterol
2 grams protein   50 mg sodium

1 starch/bread Exchange

LEMON FIZZ

This is my version of a refreshing lemonade. It's tart, tangy, and thirst quenching. Add a sprig of fresh mint for color and extra flavor.

    4 Tbsp. lemon juice
    4 Tbsp. fruit sweetener or apple juice concentrate
    2 cups club soda or seltzer
    15-20 ice cubes

Combine all of the above ingredients in blender.
Blend for 20-30 seconds. Makes 4 servings.

35 calories	0 grams fat
8 grams carb.	0 mg cholesterol
0 grams protein	30 mg sodium

1/2 fruit Exchange

ISLAND FIZZ

    2 Tbsp. Raspberry conserves (fruit juice sweetened)
    2 Tbsp. fruit juice sweetened fudge topping
    1 banana
    1/2 cup skim milk
    10 ice cubes

Combine all of the above ingredients in blender.
Blend for 20-30 seconds. Makes 1 1/2 cups. 2 servings.

145 calories	0 grams fat
35 grams carb.	1 mg cholesterol
3 grams protein	0 mg sodium

2 1/2 Fruit Exchanges

NANA STRAWBERRY SHAKE

8-10 large strawberries
2 bananas
2/3 cup skim milk
10 ice cubes

Combine the above ingredients in blender.
Blend for 20-30 seconds. Makes 2 servings.

150 calories	1 grams fat
35 grams carb.	1 mg cholesterol
4 grams protein	43 mg sodium

2 fruit Exchanges
1/3 non-fat milk Exchange

ONA ONA FUDGE SHAKE

This always brings back memories of Hawaii.

    3 Tbsp. fruit juice sweetened peanut butter
        fudge topping or classic fudge topping
    3 bananas
    2/3 cup skim milk
    10 ice cubes

Combine the above ingredients in blender.
Blend 20-30 seconds. Makes 2 large servings.

260 calories   1 grams fat
62 grams carb.   1 mg cholesterol
5 grams protein   43 mg sodium

3 fruit Exchanges
1 non-fat milk Exchange

PEACH FUZZ

What do you do with leftover fruit? Make a fuzzy drink!
I call it a fuzz because it is so cold going down, I feel
fuzzy all over.

> 2 peaches, peeled, sliced in chunks
> 1/2 cup orange juice
> 2 tsp. fruit sweetener
> > or 4 packets granulated fructose
> 1/2 tsp. vanilla
> 1 1/4 cup ice cubes

Place all ingredients in blender. Blend 20-30 seconds
makes 3 cups. 1 serving = 3/4 cup.

40 calories	0 grams fat
10 grams carb.	0 mg cholesterol
1 grams protein	0 mg sodium

2/3 fruit Exchange

INDEX

DRESSINGS

SAUCES

SALADS

SOUPS

DRINKS

JAMS

ENTREES

BREADS

SNACKS

DESSERTS

SPECIAL PRODUCTS SOURCES

DEBBIES FAMOUS GRANOLA
PO Box 5021 Niceville FL 32578
800-676-FINE
Low fat granola in 3 flavors.

FANTASTIC FOODS
Novato CA 94949
A large variety of instant foods:
refried beans, hummus,
whole wheat macaroni & cheese, falafel.

GLORIA SAMPLE & CO.
199 East Avenue
Lake Oswego OR
800-782-5881
Fruit sweetened spreads, sauces,
chutneys, marmalades, catsups, vinegars.

GUILTLESS GOURMET
512-443-4373
A great find!
Fat free tortilla chips, fat free bean dips.

HEALTH VALLEY FOODS
16100 Foothills Blvd.
Irwindale CA 91706
Fruit juice sweetened cereals, granola bars, cookies.

KOZLOWSKI FARMS
5566 Gravenstine Hiway
Forestville CA 95436
707-887-1587
Fruit sweetened spreads, preserves.

L & B KITCHENS
Waitsburg WA
509-337-8860
Wheat berry, wheat berry cookbook.

SPECIAL PRODUCTS SOURCES

GOURMET INSPIRATIONS RECIPES
have been developed
using products from the following companies:

AMERICAN SPOON FOODS
1668 Clarion Street - Box 466
Petosky MI 49770
800-222-5886
Retail and mail order
fruit sweetened spreads and topping.

BARBARA'S BAKERY PRODUCTS
3900 Cypress Crive
Petaluma CA 94954
Fruit sweetened cereals, fudge topping,
granola bars, and cookies.

CASCADIAN FARMS
311 Dillard Street
PO Box 568
Concrete WA 98273
206-853-8175
Fruit sweetener.

CASBAH
Sahara Natural Foods, Inc.
Berkeley CA 94710
Hummus, couscous, falafel.

CHUKAR CHERRIES
Prosser WA 99350
509-786-2055
Dried bing cherries.

CLEARBROOK FARMS
5514 Fair Lane
Fairfax OH 45227
800-888-3276
Fruit sweetened preserves, spreads.

SPECIAL PRODUCTS SOURCES

LEWIS HARVEY
2905 Brittan Avenue
San Carlos CA 94070
415-595-3004
Tomao Plus, Garlic Plus

MRS. STEEL'S
425 East Hector Street
Conshocken PA 19428
215-828-9430
Fudge and butterscotch toppings
sweetened with lycasin (a sugar alcohol), fruit syrups.

MYSTIC LAKES
1439 - 244th Avenue NE
Redmond WA 206-868-2029
Fruit sweetener.

SUNSPIRE: SUNLIGHT FOODS, INC.
2114 Adams Avenue
San Leandro CA 94577
Chocolate chips, vanilla chips, peanut chips;
variety of delicious candies:
English toffee, turtles, chocolate covered raisins
sweetened with barley malt.

WAX ORCHARDS
22744 Wax Orchards Road SW
Vashon WA 98070
800-634-6132
Retail and mail order.
Largest variety of fruit sweetened products.
Five flavors of fudge topping (fat free),
preserves, syrups, chutneys.
All products analyzed
for persons with diet restrictions.

ORDER FORM

To Order additional copies of any of our cookbooks, please send $12.95 per book + $2.00 shipping and handling per book to:

SWEET INSPIRATIONS INC
1420 NW GILMAN BLVD. #2258
ISSAQUAH, WA 98027

I would like to order:

_____ **SWEET INSPIRATIONS**_____ $_____
_____ **GOURMET INSPIRATIONS**_____ $_____
_____ **KIDS' STUFFIN'S**_____ $_____
Plus shipping_____ $_____
TOTAL_____ $_____

Please send to:

Name:_____

Address:_____

City/State/Zip:_____

Please designate if this is a gift and we will enclose a gift card with your greeting.

Many Thanks!
Patti Lynch